Marxist Introductions

General Editors
Raymond Williams
Steven Lukes

Also published in this series

Marxism and Law

HUGH COLLINS

Oxford New York
OXFORD UNIVERSITY PRESS

Oxford University Press, Walton Street, Oxford OX2 6DP

Oxford New York Toronto
Delhi Bombay Calcutta Madras Karachi
Petaling Jaya Singapore Hong Kong Tokyo
Nairobi Dar es Salaam Cape Town
Melbourne Auckland

and associated companies in
Beirut Berlin Ibadan Nicosia

Oxford is a trademark of Oxford University Press

First published 1982
First issued as an Oxford University Press paperback 1984
Reprinted 1986, 1987

British Library Cataloguing in Publication Data
Collins, Hugh
Marixm and philosophy.—(Marixst introductions)
1. Law.   2. Law and socialism
I. Title   II. Series
340   K357
ISBN 0–19–285144–6

Library of Congress Cataloging in Publication Data
Collins, Hugh, 1953–
Marixm and law.
(Marxist introductions)
Bibliography: p.
Includes index.
1. Law and socialism.   2. Rule of law.   I. Title
II. Series
[K357.C64 1984]   340.'115   84–7199
   ISBN 0–19–285144–6 (pbk.)

Printed in Great Britain by
Richard Clay Ltd.
Bungay, Suffolk

Preface

The idea of writing a book about Marxist theories of law first
came to me when as a student I realized to my surprise that there
were no easily comprehensible and thorough studies of the subject.
Although a decade has passed since I began to grapple with legal
philosophy, the position has hardly altered. My purpose in writing
this book, therefore, has been to provide a straightforward
account of law from a Marxist point of view. It is primarily
intended for use by students of law and jurisprudence, but it should
also be of interest to sociologists, political theorists, and persons
generally interested in Marxism. Since it is intended to be an
introductory work, inevitably some aspects of the subject have
only been considered briefly, and so the bibliography at the end
has been organized around the subjects considered in each
chapter in order to facilitate further reading and research. For
the sake of clarity in the argument I have excluded quotations
from Marx and Engels, the founders of Marxism, and more recent
authors, but references to the relevant passages will be found in
the notes and bibliography, and my debt to these writers should
be obvious.

My approach has been to describe what I believe to be the most
coherent insights into law put forward by Marxists and then to
subject them to criticism. Ultimately, therefore, the book rejects
or severely qualifies many of the Marxist analyses of law, but I
hope that in the process the strengths and weaknesses of this
point of view have been clarified.

I am grateful to many of my teachers, colleagues, and friends
who have assisted me and offered helpful criticisms of earlier
drafts of the book. In particular I am indebted to: C. Boyle, P.
Cameron, D. Galligan, Y. Onuma, C. Sampford, E. Simonoff, D.
Sugerman, and J. Willmott. I am also grateful to Sir Otto Kahn-
Freund for initially encouraging me to take on this project, and it
is a cause of great sadness to me that he did not live to see its
completion. R. Unger carries the responsibility of having first
taught me about social theory and law, but he is absolved from
any connection with this particular work since he always advised

against it; I hope that I have evaded many of the pitfalls which he pointed out to me. On a material level I am grateful to the British Academy for assisting me financially. Finally, but most important of all, I am heavily indebted to H. L. A. Hart for his advice, criticism, and encouragement. Together with many others who are interested in theoretical studies of law, I am deeply grateful for the inspiration provided by his work. Indubitably he has saved me from many grave errors. I hope that I have eliminated the defects which he and others have pointed out to me, but I fear that much is left of which they would disapprove. Naturally, the responsibility for the remaining errors rests with me.

Oxford, 1982   Hugh Collins

Contents

1. The Marxist Approach to Law

The principal aim of Marxist jurisprudence is to criticize the centrepiece of liberal political philosophy, the ideal called the Rule of Law. Although this undertaking constitutes a mere fragment of the Marxist tradition of critical social theory, today it is regarded as a vital element. Never before have Marxists devoted so much energy to the investigation of the nature and functions of legal systems. Their efforts merge into the general purpose of Marxism which is to mount a sustained offensive against the existing organizations of power in modern society. By exposing the structures of domination and subverting the beliefs and values which sustain them, Marxists seek to pave the way towards a revolutionary social transformation. Within this programme, the theory of law assumes an important place. Marxists examine the real nature of law in order to reveal its functions in the organizations of power and to undermine the pervasive legitimating ideology in modern industrial societies known as the Rule of Law.

This contumacious purpose of Marxist jurisprudence sets it apart from other modern schools of legal philosophy. The typical legal theory dispensed in law schools presents descriptions of law, analyses of legal concepts, and inquiries into the demands of justice, based upon assumptions about the legitimate authority of the power which is exercised through the institutions of a modern legal system. But since Marxism is bent upon the overthrow of the existing apparatus of domination, its objectives in the study of law differ markedly, and consequently not all the levels and directions of its jurisprudence are encompassed by standard definitions of the subject. Nevertheless there is sufficient common ground for Marxists to offer contrasting interpretations of legal phenomena which are examined by other philosophies of law. Perhaps inevitably the underlying differences in political viewpoint have led to the development of an antagonistic relationship between Marxism and the remaining schools of jurisprudence.[1] Unfortunately during the course of bitter attacks upon Marxist

1

legal theory, its positions have often been distorted, so one of my purposes here is to attempt to set the record straight.

In addition to this conflict between political ideals, another factor has almost certainly contributed to the asperity of the debate with Marxist jurisprudence. Marxism is often closely associated with Communist governments since these countries claim Marxism as their official ideology, so disapproval of Marxist jurisprudence is equated in the West with patriotic sentiment and the vilification of one-party states. It will, however, become apparent in later chapters that I believe it is erroneous to associate the values of Communist states closely with Marxist social theory. The links between the two are problematic, and certainly weaker than is commonly supposed. Accordingly I will not pay special attention to the laws found in those Communist states. Nor will I be especially interested in the jurisprudence emanating from those countries, for despite its great bulk, that literature fails to make a significant contribution to the Marxist analysis of law.[2]

But if Marxism is not the same as Communism, or to be precise, if Communist states cannot reasonably claim to be based squarely upon Marxist principles and to be their authoritative interpreters, then what is Marxism? Clearly we must address ourselves to this question before progressing to the details of the Marxist theory of law.

(1) What is Marxism?

Marxism is a theory about the meaning of history. However aimless the wanderings of mankind may have seemed to others, Marxists have discerned a regular evolutionary pattern controlling the human condition. Behind the complexity and particularity of isolated events human civilization has been gradually moving towards the goal of history. Once the direction of this progress and the reasons for social change are perceived, then the secrets of the future can be glimpsed. According to Marxism the meaning of history is that man's destiny lies in the creation of a Communist society where men will experience a higher stage of being amounting to the realization of true freedom.

Of course the notion that history represents an evolutionary pattern and contains intimations of futurity is not exclusively Marxist. Many religions and metaphysical systems of speculative thought subscribe to similar beliefs. Nor is a prediction of the coming of a utopian society a doctrine peculiar to Marxism. During the Middle Ages in Europe, and even in modern times, the imminent arrival of the millennium and the establishment of a community of saints has been constantly heralded. During the nineteenth century, in the period when Marxism was originally devised, philosophers and cranks frequently published tracts proposing the creation of utopian societies based upon communal living and novel moral codes. What then, if not a belief that history has a meaning or a prediction of the arrival of utopia, makes Marxism a distinctive set of ideas? What are the principal tenets of this interpretation of history? These questions serve as a convenient starting-point for an investigation into the Marxist approach to law, both in its theoretical dimension and with regard to its programmes for political action.

They are not, however, questions which can be answered briefly in straightforward terms. One reason why quick responses are unavailable lies in the fact that there have been a great variety of Marxist theories. A host of schools, all with their own distinctive contributions, have marched under the banner of Marxism. Many of these movements such as the Frankfurt School have developed theoretical positions which bear faint resemblance to those held by early Marxists. It is therefore hard to judge whether they merit a place in a book about the Marxist approach to law. Even major figures in the history of the world such as Mao Tse-tung who have claimed to be Marxists have had their credentials seriously doubted, and frequently with good reason. So an answer to the question of what the principal doctrines of Marxism are can only be supplied once a decision about whom to treat as Marxists has been reached. Plainly some guidance can be provided from the terminology by which thinkers label themselves, but we should be aware of the pitfall of inflating the ambit of the Marxist tradition so far that it incorporates contradictory insights.

Another possible touchstone for a definition of Marxism could be consistency with the writings of Karl Marx. He originally formulated many of the distinctive insights of Marxism and his name was subsequently given to the whole tradition. The earliest published work in which Marx crystallized his social and political theory was the *Communist Manifesto* 1848. This short polemical tract, written in conjunction with his lifelong friend Frederick Engels, helps to define the parameters of Marxism. In addition there are many other writings, a number of them left in manuscript form during Marx's lifetime, which provide a body of literature by which to assess the authenticity of views purporting to be Marxist. Yet this standard will prove unsatisfactorily narrow if some indication of the wide range of Marxist theorizing about law is sought. Moreover, consistency with Marx's works is an unworkable criterion, for Marx sometimes contradicted himself and there are ambiguities in his writings. Indeed, many of the debates within Marxism open with scholastic disputes about the meaning of obscure passages, or labour over the reconciliation of apparently contradictory pronouncements.

There seems no alternative, therefore, if we are to proceed further with an investigation of the Marxist approach towards law, but to offer a tentative definition of Marxism. Naturally any proposal will take into account both Marx's writings and the content of works claiming to be Marxist. The definition of Marxism offered here will inevitably be controversial, but I believe that it is possible to identify an underlying unity in the Marxist vision of history. This thread binding the Marxist tradition together can be perceived in two elements of the theory: first, a common methodology for deciphering the meaning of history, and, second, a prediction that the destiny of mankind lies in a Communist society. I shall consider these two themes in turn.

On the matter of methodology, the outstanding characteristic of Marxism is its close affinity to the methods of the natural sciences such as chemistry or biology. In order to establish the meaning of history Marx insisted that we should scrutinize the past to discover the causes of social change and the underlying currents of progress much like a scientist conducting an experiment. Whereas other kinds of historicism had looked for mystical signs, spiritual revelation, or relied upon higher faculties of reason to predict the path of civilization, Marx rejected all such speculative metaphysics. He insisted that the source of social change lay in the world itself, in the material conditions of life. There were no transcendental forces controlling events on the planet, nor was history dependent upon a process of the resolution of deep structures of ideals and values espoused by men. For Marx the source of social change lay in the material circumstances in which men found themselves and how they responded to their predicament. It followed that his method for constructing an interpretation of the meaning of history lay in a close examination of the material basis of prior civilizations in order to discover how men had reacted to their conditions and to identify the causes of instability which eventually led to successive transformations of that society.

So Marxists insist that their methodology is scientific because it looks at observable, or at least observed, data in order to support a thesis about the meaning of history. It is also scientific in the sense that it holds that all social phenomena should be explicable within the general framework. In principle the theory can be modified or amended in the light of contrary evidence. Many critics of Marxism would argue that the conclusions reached by the early Marxists such as Marx, Engels, and Lenin have been raised to the status of irrefutable dogma so that no amount of contrary evidence can rebut their views, in which case any claim by Marxists to approximate their methodology to that of the empirical sciences would be misleading. Indubitably this charge of a betrayal of the standards of truth used in empirical sciences is well founded against some Marxists, particularly those writing and working under repressive political regimes. Yet as an indictment against the whole Marxist tradition it is not convincing. There have been many historians, sociologists, and political scientists who have followed the Marxist analysis but who have offered amendments and additions where they have found the established views inadequate or false. In the course of this book we shall see how the Marxist attitude towards legal institutions has been contested and refined over numerous generations, and that is sufficient proof that the blanket condemnation of Marxism as unscientific and dogmatic is wrong and does not withstand empirical examination itself.

Nevertheless, the correspondence between Marxism and the natural sciences cannot be exact for two reasons. In the first place — and this is a theoretical obstacle recognized by all modern social theories — the concepts which we use to analyse social phenomena always seem more contestable than the categories of natural science. Much of the debate in the social sciences focuses on the utility of the concepts themselves, whereas there is a greater measure of consensus in the natural sciences over how to establish strong evidence to support a hypothesis. To take one example: Marxists describe modern western societies as capitalist. Certain features of the economic infrastructure and social stratifications are identified as common characteristics of all these countries. Yet it is equally possible to insist that the differences in their attributes outweigh their similarities. Whereas one country might rely heavily upon agriculture and manufacturing for the production of wealth, another might specialize in advanced technology. At the same time these societies might possess considerable divergences in their occupational groups and political parties. To say that modern western societies are all capitalist is therefore to force a common classification upon disparate phenomena. It might be better to distinguish between different kinds of capitalist societies such as finance and monopoly capitalism, western and eastern capitalism, and post-industrial societies. What is controversial in the social sciences therefore is the soundness of the conceptual categories which are used. Can they be objectively valid or at least generally accepted as the appropriate criteria of similarity and difference? In the natural sciences, in contrast, there is seldom disagreement about the appropriate units of measurement such as molecules, temperatures, or elements. Any debate tends to centre on inferences about causal links between the agreed data which have been observed. All of this is elementary to modern philosophers, but when Marx was writing in the middle of the nineteenth century there were great hopes for bringing the entire methodology of natural science to social theory which led Marx to make many assertions about the scientific nature of his studies. Ironically, instead of the study of society being gradually subsumed under the natural sciences, it is now realized that many of the theoretical obstacles to simple empiricism experienced in the social sciences apply equally to the natural sciences, so the fact that many concepts are uncontroversial in biology or chemistry does not mean that they are incontestable.

There is a second reason for distancing Marxism from the methodology of the natural sciences. A distinctive aspect of Marxist social thought lies in its conception of the relationship between theory and practice. The point is that the observer of a society is a part of that society himself. His writings and theoretical conclusions also form part of the total sum of knowledge available within that community. It is possible, therefore, that the theory will influence behaviour if it is consciously accepted and followed. In other words, theory does not merely describe social practice; it may also change it.

This relationship between theory and practice stands in marked contrast to the natural sciences. As far as we know a chemist's or biologist's conclusions about the causal nexus between physical phenomena will not induce those objects to react differently. Similarly, it is rare for sociologists outside the Marxist tradition to recognize the potential effect of their own theoretical work upon the subject of their studies. Yet this relationship is central to the methodology of Marxism, particularly in connection with class consciousness. To define a group, delineate its boundaries, and articulate its aspirations, enables the members of that group to develop a higher degree of group-consciousness. Individuals can better identify with a corporate body once it has been rendered visible through descriptive writings and polemics. The strength of political movements depends to a large extent upon the degree to which supporters are prepared to perceive themselves as part of a group with a strong sense of solidarity; that perception itself augments the degree of cohesiveness within the group. Marxists are aware of this significant effect of their doctrines especially with regard to class consciousness. They understand that theoretical work can amount to a kind of political practice designed to bring about social change.

Once this connection between theory and practice is established then it becomes obvious why Marxists are tempted to fall into standard patterns of discourse which have the appearance of dogma. Since theory may influence the course of history, it cannot be value-free, nor should it seek to be so, for that would constitute irrational blindness to the consequences of one's actions. Concepts and categories of social theory such as the notion of social class are not only contestable because of the aptness of their description of existing phenonema, but also because they may affect the behaviour of those groups being observed. Some Marxists have attached such importance to the preservation of a theoretical analysis conducive to the maximization of class-consciousness and intensification of conflict that the original fidelity to the empirical sciences has been lost behind the mindless repetition of hallowed rhetoric. There may indeed be an insoluble tension between the commitment to empiricism and the recognition of a complex relationship between theory and practice. But the intractability of these philosophical issues should not provide licence for the propagation of implausible dogma.

We can summarize the methodology common to Marxists as a combination of empirical investigation and a realization of the intimate relationship between observer and observed or the effect of theory upon practice. I shall have to add to the complexity of this brief account of methodology in the course of this book, particularly in the context of the Marxist explanation of the origins and nature of ideologies, but this simplified general survey should suffice to indicate the distinctive features at the core of the Marxist approach to history.

The second distinguishing mark of the Marxist tradition is its belief that the destiny of mankind lies in Communism. What does this prediction signify? Marx argued in the *Communist Manifesto* that modern society is based upon a capitalist economy. This system is composed of some persons who own the means of production such as factories or land, and these capitalists employ the mass of the population to produce goods to be sold at a profit. Modern society is roughly divided into these two social classes, the owners of the means of production and the proletariat who work for them. Marx predicted that eventually a political struggle would occur as a result of the conflict of interest between the polarized classes of capitalist society. The proletariat would seize power through a revolution and create a new kind of classless society in which the means of production would be owned in common by the entire community. In addition the social division of labour under which men perform tasks at someone else's beck and call would be abolished. Everyone would then experience true freedom for they would have control over every aspect of their lives. There would be not only an alteration in the organization of political power and the production of wealth but also a transformation in the nature of men themselves for they would attain a higher state of being.

Marx thought that capitalism was the penultimate stage in the process of history. The next and final phase would be Communism, though the timing of the transition was indeterminate, and there would be a period of transition. The course of events would depend not only on economic conditions but also in part upon political action and theoretical work. No wonder Marx regarded his breakthrough as tremendously important! Since theory affects practice, he believed that his solution to the riddle of the meaning of history actually hastened the transition to the utopian destiny of mankind.

This is the essence of Marx's vision of Communism. It is shared by most Marxists. As capitalism continues to resist major transformation of the kind envisaged by Marx, optimism about the inevitability of the advent of the revolution gives way to an emphasis on the need for direct political action verging on opportunism. These debates among Marxists about the appropriate strategy for hastening the crisis of capitalism forge serious divisions between political wings of the Marxist tradition. Nevertheless all factions continue to accept Marx's prediction of the origins and nature of a Communist society. The unity of Marxist thought lies in its common methodology together with this shared vision of the transformation of capitalist society into Communism. I shall treat these principles as my guide for including thinkers within the Marxist tradition and for judging the degree of fidelity to the mainstream of Marxism contained in competing interpretations of law.

(2) Is there a Marxist theory of law?

It has often been remarked that there is no Marxist theory of law. At first sight this is a strange assertion for it is in the nature of Marxism as a general theory of the evolution of societies that it will pass comment on significant institutions such as the law. Admittedly the main thrust of Marxist analysis is directed towards the economic infrastructure and the organizations of power in a community. That emphasis stems naturally from Marx's insight that the source of social change and the revelation of the destiny of man can only be discovered from the material circumstances of life and how man has responded to them. It follows that law is not a central focus of concern for Marxists. Neither is law a prominent analytical concept of comparable importance to social class or capitalism for example. Nevertheless legal systems are of considerable interest to Marxists because of the part they play in different social formations such as feudalism or capitalism. Marxists cannot deny the importance of some of the functions performed by legal institutions, but essentially their interest in law is tangential to a predominant focus on the general mode of social organization and the material circumstances in which men are placed. In so far as law has played a part in these decisive factors in the evolution of society then it has been of concern to Marxists.

In fact only a few have troubled themselves to examine law in any detail. For the most part discussions have been restricted to cursory remarks forming a section in work of a broader compass. Thus legal rules are often cited as a means of illustrating the course of political struggles and the evolution of social formations. But the nature of legal institutions themselves remains an unexplored terrain. Apart from extremely recent literature there are only two major works devoted exclusively to the formulation of a Marxist theory of law. Both were composed in the early part of this century. The first was Karl Renner's treatise about the relationship between law and social change, called *The Institutions of Private Law and their Social Functions* (1904).[3] Slightly later, after the 1917 Revolution in the USSR a Soviet jurist named Evgeny Pashukanis outlined a more general theory of law.[4] Recently there has been a flurry of articles and books devoted to Marxist studies of law. They have found their inspiration in historical studies and novel theoretical positions emanating from French and German Marxists. In addition Cain and Hunt have conveniently amassed extracts from the scattered writings of Marx and Engels on law in a book,[5] though it is evident from that collection that neither of the founders of Marxism ever developed a systematic approach to law.

The paucity of Marxist jurisprudence until modern times is probably largely a result of the materialist emphasis of Marxism. Since the primary focus rests on the economy and the corresponding power relations within a society, law is treated as a peripheral concern. Even then it is usually relegated to the position of a relatively unproblematic sector of the State scarcely worthy of detailed consideration. There is, however, a second reason for the absence of a Marxist theory of law in a highly developed form which goes to the roots of our perception of legal institutions.

To demand a general theory of law from a Marxist is to ask him to run the risk of falling prey to what can be termed the fetishism of law. In a later chapter I shall consider the origins and significance of the phenomenon of legal fetishism, but it is necessary to introduce the idea now in order to understand why Marxists have avoided the task of formulating a general theory of law. What is meant by the fetishism of law? In simple terms it is the belief that legal systems are an essential component of social order and civilization. This belief is a pervasive feature of social and political theories outside the Marxist tradition. It serves as the foundation for most liberal political theory. In addition, this notion underlies all the important general theories of law which are in currency today. Because Marxism does not subscribe to the fetishism of law it also resists the directions of speculative thought which seek to provide a general theory of law. We can understand this point more clearly if the attributes of legal fetishism are examined in greater detail.

There are three features of legal fetishism which should be highlighted. In the first place there is the thesis that a legal order is necessary for social order: unless there is a system of laws designed to ensure compliance with a set of rules which define rights and entitlements then no civilization is possible; if laws and legal institutions were abolished anarchy would immediately break out. H. L. A. Hart expresses this idea with his claim that there must be a minimum content of law.[6] Unless there are rules governing ownership of property and enforcing prohibitions against physical violence, he says, society would be impossible. If a legal system, or at least some kind of coercive system, failed to provide such rules, the community would disintegrate. For those who fetishize law, legal rules are at the centre of social life, forming the basis for peaceful social intercourse. Like other norms such as the conventions on which linguistic communication is based, legal rules provide the foundation for exchanges, reliance, safety, privacy, and satisfy numerous other perennial human wants. It can be added that the greater the sophistication of the legal system, the more effective it will be in the satisfaction of those wants, and the more truly it will be like law. Thus Hart speaks of a transition from purely customary rules of the pre-legal world to the authentic legal order of modern society which has rules to cover all eventualities including mechanisms for altering the existing laws.[7]

A second contention of legal fetishism is that law is a unique phenomenon which constitutes a discrete focus of study. Legal systems are not simply types of a broader species of systems of power, but they possess distinctive characteristics. In particular, modern jurisprudence identifies three exclusive features of legal systems. First, there are regular patterns of institutional arrangements associated with law such as the division between a legislature and a judiciary. Second, lawyers communicate with each other through a distinctive mode of discourse, though the exact nature of legal reasoning remains controversial. Third, legal systems are distinguished from simple exercises of force by one group over another; for legal rules also function as normative guides to behaviour which individuals follow regardless of the presence or absence of officials threatening to impose sanctions for failing to comply with the law. Together these three features of law, its institutional framework, its methodology, and its normativity, are considered to make law a unique phenomenon. They constitute the background for the whole enterprise of modern jurisprudence which seeks to provide a general theory of law. Whereas the first thesis of legal fetishism encouraged us to believe that law contains the answers to the problem of the origin of civilization and thus made a general theory of law of interest, the second feature of legal fetishism, a belief in the uniqueness of law, suggests that it is possible to isolate legal phenomena and to study their nature. A final aspect of legal fetishism makes a general theory of law not only interesting and possible but also crucial to political theory.

This third feature is the doctrine of the Rule of Law. The meaning of this idea is complex; considerable attention will be devoted to its connotations and implications in the final chapter. For the time being a crude approximation to its meaning will suffice to demonstrate its link to legal fetishism. The core principle of the doctrine is that political power should be exercised according to rules announced in advance. A political system is analogous to a game: it is only fair to give prior notice of the rules to all the participants and then to insist that everyone abide by them even in adversity. The Rule of Law does not require that the laws should have any particular kind of content, but simply that they should constrain the weak and powerful alike. Such a political principle inhibits arbitrary despots and authoritarian oligarchies from dispossessing citizens of their liberties without cause shown. A substantial portion of the motivation behind the construction of general theories of law lies in a desire to demonstrate that the Rule of Law is a realistic ideal. What has to be proven therefore is that the laws of a society can be identified and then applied impartially. A general theory of law hopes to provide criteria by which laws can be distinguished from other phenomena and then explain how legal rules can be interpreted and applied by judges independently of concern for their own or their friends' material interests. Such a theory is plainly crucial to styles of political legitimation which rest predominately on the ideal of the Rule of Law.

Marxists have rejected these three aspects of legal fetishism. They concede that such ideas represent a persuasive interpretation of reality found in modern society. Few would doubt the important role of law in preventing the disintegration of social order or restricting authoritarian governments. Yet Marxists claim that legal fetishism embodies a distorted image of reality which must be unmasked. To begin with, the notion that society rests on law is too simplistic. It is implausible to think that without law everyone would be at each other's throat, or would use superior physical force to take another's possessions. It is much more likely that informal standards of behaviour based on reciprocity would permit an elementary form of stable community to exist. Clearly there is a subtle relationship between the function of laws and informal customs in constituting the normative basis for a peaceful and prosperous society which will not be revealed if an assumption about the necessity and priority of law is adopted. Growing from that insight, Marxists portray the heavy dependence of organizations of power in modern society upon law as the result of a specific historic conjuncture of circumstances, and argue further that the important role of law today in maintaining social order is not an immutable feature of human civilization in the future.

Equally Marxists deny that there is a special and distinctive phenomenon which we can term law. Because Marxism has approached law tangentially, treating it as one aspect of a variety of political and social arrangements concerned with the manipulation of power and the consolidation of modes of production of wealth, there has been no commitment towards an identification of the unique qualities of legal institutions. Of course the term law is conventionally used to refer to particular kinds of systems of rules which find their paradigm in modern societies, but Marxism has not felt bound by the parameters of linguistic usage when considering law. What is more important for a Marxist is to notice how laws or law-like institutions serve particular functions within a social formation. The focus is switched from proposing a definition and drawing up of lists of functions of law to devising an explanation of the functions which laws together with other social institutions help to perform in particular historical contexts. Guided by the emphasis upon materialism, Marxists avoid assumptions about the uniqueness of legal phenomena or their essence, and so they rarely offer a general theory of law, Pashukanis being the obvious exception.

The final aspect of legal fetishism, the doctrine of the Rule of Law, illustrates one of the functions which laws help to perform, and as such it has been of great interest to Marxists. Since legal rules can inhibit the arbitrary exercise of power, even if their control is precarious, law can contribute an important dimension to political philosophies seeking to explain or justify the existing structures of political domination on the ground that the powerful are constrained by the demands of due process of law. The ideal of the Rule of Law encapsulates this legitimizing function of legal systems. The bulk of western jurisprudence uses the Rule of Law doctrine as a standard by which to judge the success or desirability of a general theory of law.[8] It is crucial for these legal philosophers to demonstrate the superiority of their approach towards the problem of the identification of the laws of a particular legal system because they can then argue that they have proved the coherence of the predominant legitimating ideology of power in liberal society. Marxists, however, are obviously uninterested in putting forward a theory of their own, for their purpose is to challenge rather than defend the present organization of power. Accordingly you will not find here those elaborate analyses of the structures of legal systems which parade as legal theory in the law schools. Nevertheless the Rule of Law and the function of law in modern theories of the legitimation of power remain of vital interest to Marxists in their search for a critical understanding of the complexities of modern social systems. Therefore, a general theory of law in the conventional mode would be an anathema to Marxism, though legal phenomena must constitute a central focus of inquiry.

In summary, general theories of law are predicated on a belief in the nature of law which can be termed legal fetishism. Marxists reject such a belief and it follows that they are not inclined to develop a general theory of law as an end in itself. Nevertheless much remains for Marxists to say about law. This book will be focused on three questions which are central to the Marxist interpretation of history.

First we can ask what are the characteristic functions of legal institutions? In order to do so, we need not assume that law is a unique phenomenon. There may be hazy borderlines between legal rules and other kinds of social rules such as morality, custom, and etiquette. What we can look at are the functions of institutions conventionally treated as legal. This direction of the inquiry will be restricted in one respect for I have excluded any discussion of Public International Law which governs the relations between nation states. I have not made this omission on the ground that Public International Law is not law, for such a decision would be one motivated by an aspect of legal fetishism. The reason for the exclusion is rather that the functions performed by law in an international sphere are likely to be very different from the role of law in governing relations between individuals and groups within one society, so to discuss Public International Law would broaden the field considerably, and I have preferred to concentrate my energies on laws within legal systems.

The second question is whether law is necessary for human civilization? To some extent the answer to this question builds on the insights afforded by investigating the functions of law. Yet a look at the need for law raises broader issues about the origins of social order. In particular it poses the question of whether or not law will exist in a Communist society? Perhaps the most notorious pronouncement ever made by Marxists about law is that it will disappear in a Communist society. This claim is ridiculed as blind utopianism. Clearly the strength of such criticism rests on the first aspect of legal fetishism, the belief that law is necessary for any civilization to flourish. We will see in Chapter 5 that in fact the Marxist position is more subtle than is commonly supposed. It may be appropriate to add here that the fact that self-proclaimed Communist countries have vast legal systems cannot in any way negate the theory about the withering away of law. Whatever the true nature of such regimes, they are plainly far removed from the conception of Communism which the classic theorists of Marxism had in mind. If anything the presence of laws in those societies proves that they are not Communist rather than disposing of the Marxist theory that law is unnecessary.

The final question is what precisely is the political practice of Marxists towards law in modern society? How should they comprehend and respond to ideas such as the Rule of Law? To what extent should Marxists be concerned with legality and feel under an obligation to obey the law? These questions will be dealt with in the last chapter which examines the relationship between theory and political practice in this field. It is there that the reasons for the antagonism between Marxism and the Rule of Law will be discussed.

My answer to the first question will occupy the next three chapters. This examination of the functions of law is lengthy not only because of its complexity but also because it must be situated within a broader study of social institutions for, as we have already noted, Marxists reject from the outset the notion that law is a unique and distinct phenomenon. So the functions of law will be explained in the context of a wider view of the way in which societies are held together, how they are structured, and the causes of social change. In short, we must start with the Marxist interpretation of history.

2. Law as an Instrument of Class Oppression

The general theory of Marxism is called historical materialism. It explains how social systems work, and why transformations in societies take place. The theory provides the concepts and methodology for a Marxist analysis of every aspect of a society including its legal system. A precise, detailed formulation of historical materialism acceptable to all strands within the Marxist tradition is probably unobtainable. Yet there is one work which has often been treated as a definitive text. This is Marx's Preface to an essay entitled 'A Contribution to the Critique of Political Economy'.[1] The Preface is certainly important and my account of the Marxist theory of law takes it as a starting-point, but I shall not use it as my sole guide. One reason is that the Preface merely presents in a highly condensed form some of the conclusions reached in Marx's earlier work like 'The German Ideology'[2] where they were elaborated and illustrated at length; it would be foolish not to look at those other classic texts for guidance. Another reason is that in this book I shall be concerned not only with Marx's own vision of history but also later diverse interpretations of historical materialism which may not prove to be entirely consistent with the formulations in the Preface. So I shall commence by outlining elements of historical materialism pertinent to law which have been common to various strands of the Marxist tradition, but my account may not tally precisely with the views of any one author. This account is intended only as a preliminary description of the Marxist theory of law which will be progressively refined in the course of the book.

(1) Elements of Historical Materialism

When one studies the evolution of human societies, the role of conscious action in the determination of events presents a central theoretical problem. Are we free to create our own history and to pursue cherished ideals, or are we programmed since birth by our biological make-up and the environment in which we live to follow certain evolutionary patterns? How far is the sense of choice which men experience when participating in historical events illusory? It is possible to make a crude division among the orientations of social theories into those which credit the human mind with the ability to transcend the circumstances of existence and to make their own history, and those theories which reduce human behaviour to determined patterns of evolution conditioned by external factors, like the availability of food, and internal biological needs such as nutrient and sexual intercourse. The former view may be termed idealism and the latter is usually called materialism.

In the history of social thought it has been rare for a theorist to remain faithful to one extreme or other. Marx was no exception. The core of his formulations of the theory of historical materialism contains a rejection of the largely idealistic philosophies of his contemporaries and mentors in Germany, but at the same time Marx distanced himself from any simple version of materialism. What remains most problematic in the interpretation of his writings is precisely how he attempted to reconcile a fundamental orientation towards materialism with the acknowledged importance of conscious action in the construction and transformation of societies. This problem is particularly acute in the analysis of law, for legal institutions and rules are often perceived as purposive human creations, the products of deliberate conscious action. In modern society where the predominant form of law is a complex regulatory code, this purposive, artificial aspect of the nature of law is especially apparent. The theory of historical materialism has to explain how these consciously created laws are ultimately determined by material circumstances.

What are the relevant material circumstances? In the Preface Marx insisted that we look for the material circumstances which are vital to sustain even the most elementary forms of social life. Men always have to satisfy certain biological needs for the reproduction of the species such as food, clothing, and shelter. These requirements are met by the exploitation of natural resources through the use of the available technologies. During the course of production men enter into social relations, and Marx reasoned that these *relations of production* are the basic constituents of any society.

The form of the relations of production will depend on the nature of the available natural resources and the knowledge of technologies for exploiting them, the two together being described by Marx as *the forces of production*. A simple example is provided by the earliest kind of human society which was the group of nomadic hunters. The elusiveness of the prey combined with the limited technology of wooden and stone weapons entails that successful hunting would generally have required the co-operation of a group of hunters. We may suppose that this group entered into an arrangement governing the procedure for hunting and afterwards for the division of the spoils. The form of this arrangement, the relations of production, will always be linked functionally to a combination of the technology and the nature of the resource to be exploited, in this case those forces of production being the primitive weapons and the abundance of wild life. Unless the arrangement satisfies the needs of the hunting community to co-operate in order to use the available technologies and natural resources efficiently, it will probably never arise, or at least be very quickly abandoned.

Having established the intimate connection of the relations of production with the material world, Marx then suggested in the Preface that all the social institutions of a community including its structures of political authority and its laws arise from and adapt themselves to the nature of the relations of production. Thus laws are determined in their form and content by the relations of production, or, to use another Marxist term, by the *material base*. Indeed, if a conflict develops between the political and legal *super-structure* and the requirements of the relations of production then severe dislocation will result. For example, if in the community of hunters some rule was announced forbidding hunting in groups, then in order to avoid starvation either an entirely new mode of production would have to be discovered, or more likely there would be a revolution against the authority which was attempting to impose the rule.

The determinative influence of the material base does not halt at social institutions. Marx argued further that even ideas, values, beliefs, and superstitions are all dependent on a particular form of relations of production. He referred to them all as ideologies, thus signifying that they were dependent on the material circumstances through which men experienced the world. The corollary of this view is that in the long run men do not have the freedom to develop ideologies in any directions which appear to them to be just or true, but rather the history of ideas must be examined as a series of responses to transformations within the relations of production. Naturally, this material determinism applies equally to legal doctrinal thought and legal reasoning. Both the institutional framework of the legal system and the substance of the legal rules are ultimately determined by the relations of production.

It follows as well that historical materialism establishes a permanent barrier between itself and any idealist interpretation of history. Marxists argue from their materialist premises that the real source of transformations in societies is not to be discovered in altered ideas and world-views but rather in disjunctions within the economic base. In other words, the evolution of social formations such as capitalism cannot simply be explained as a result of revised systems of values or the propagation of new systems of religious beliefs. According to the theory of historical materialism, the catalyst behind the evolution of societies lies in conflicts between the forces of production and the relations of production which produce revolutionary ideas.

How do conflicts engendering social change arise? It is evident that the level of sophistication of technologies does not remain constant. The natural ingenuity of men leads to an accumulation of knowledge about mechanics, engineering, and thermodynamics which permits more efficient exploitation of natural resources. Changes in the forces of production as a result of the invention of new technologies may not be satisfactorily accommodated within the existing relations of production. Thus the machines invented for spinning thread could only be utilized if workers were introduced into centralized places of work instead of the raw material being farmed out to individual households. The new relations of production in the factory provided the opportunity to satisfy the functional requirements of the new technology.

Signs of pressures for change can be noticed in challenges to social rules including laws which govern the existing relations of production. These rules may inhibit or fetter the development of new production arrangements more suited to the exploitation of the forces of production. If so, then those groups or social classes who seek to use the novel technology will engage in political struggles in an attempt to reform the laws so that they become compatible with efficient relations of production. Thus history may be interpreted as a series of phases of struggles between social classes as each new set of production arrangements seeks to gain a foothold in the permissible range of social practices. In the event of a major alteration in the relations of production brought about by a revolutionary political movement, a whole new mode of production will emerge with its corresponding political and legal superstructures.

An example of this revolutionary cycle which Marx often had in mind was the transition from feudalism through a number of intermediate stages to capitalism. The feudal laws of tenure governing rights and duties associated with land were appropriate to the agricultural modes of production of pre-capitalist societies because they ensured social order and at the same time the efficient use of existing technologies. The essential pattern was the exchange of services by the serf in return for military protection by the lord and tenure of arable land from which the serf could feed himself and his family. The serf was in effect tied to the land because he could not decline the arrangement. Similarly the lord was committed to the retention of the lands indefinitely. Thus the laws controlling tenure of land were inconsistent with the use of property as a capital asset to be bought and sold freely on the market and then to be exploited according to the directions of the owner by wage-labourers. As a consequence the law relating to tenure became a focus of political struggle between on the one hand groups protecting the feudal mode of production such as the aristocracy and on the other hand those classes like the bourgeoisie and landed gentry who sought to establish a new commercial society. When these social classes eventually resorted to violent conflict during the English revolution in the seventeenth century in order to establish new relations of production they naturally passed legislation to abolish the remnants of the laws still supporting the feudal system of property relations. When the wars were over and a final political settlement was established, the position was consolidated by the enactment of the Tenures (Abolition) Act 1660.[3] Thus old laws which placed fetters upon the extension of novel relations of production were overthrown by a new ruling class once it had seized power.

As well as explaining the content of the laws of any historical epoch, the theory of historical materialism aims to explicate the various forms in which law emerges. It should be possible to demonstrate a determinate relationship between the material basis of various social formations and the form of their laws. There will be links between certain modes of production and a customary informal style of law. Similarly historical materialism links the development of modern relations of production to the form of modern legal systems with their panoply of courts, legis-lature, and lawyers. It explains why the political action which abolished tenures in England in 1660 took the form of a statute to be enforced by a complicated system of law courts, rather than, say, a gradual transition of meaning in a set of customary rules.

The theory of historical materialism therefore argues that legal phenomena are essentially superstructural, dependent for their form and content upon determining forces emanating from the economic basis of society. This metaphor of base and super-structure has usually been adopted as the starting-point for an explanation of the nature of law in Marxist writings. The various patterns and stages of the evolution of societies progress according to forces within the mode of production, and the law merely exists on the periphery of these developments both consolidating forms of the relations of production and inhibiting any challenges to the social system. Although this thesis of historical materialism will have to be modified substantially when a deeper look at it is undertaken, its broad orientation of locating the legal system as an epiphenomenon of the real material world will remain a guiding thread for the Marxist analysis of law.

(2) Crude Materialism and Class Instrumentalism

Although Marx frequently referred to law in his mature work, he never pursued the analytical framework laid down in the Preface with regard to legal systems. He concentrated his energies where his theory indicated that the key to social formations could be discovered, in the economic relations of production. His discussions of law such as the references to the Factory Acts in 'Capital' were developed in order to support his analysis of the mode of prod-uction and do not present a mature understanding of legal phenomena.[4]

Nevertheless I think that his fragmentary remarks combined with general principles of historical materialism can provide the outlines for a Marxist theory of law which is broadly consistent with Marx's own writings. Before attempting this reconstruction myself, I shall turn to the works of eminent Marxists, especially Engels and Lenin, to consider how they interpreted law in the light of the principles of historical materialism. Their views may be crudely divided into two camps, one veering close to a simple materialist analysis of historical change and the other emphasizing instead the importance of social classes for understanding the place of law in a social formation.

To begin with, in the last quarter of the nineteenth century, the metaphors contained in the Preface recited above dominated the Marxist analysis of law. The key was found in the base and super-structure idea. It was said that law was a reflection of the economic base; the form and content of laws corresponded to the dominant mode of production. Thus informal laws of tenure were the product of the feudal mode of production, and modern legal systems with their codes of laws and a specialized judiciary to interpret them reflected capitalist relations of production. Some support for this analysis of law was given by Engels. He lived on for more than twenty years after the death of Marx, and during that period he frequently repeated similar formulas in correspon-dence and published works. Laws, he argued, corresponded to the general economic condition of a society, and expressed or reflected the relations of production.[5] This mode of analysis has been termed 'economism' or crude materialism because of the extreme emphasis placed upon the determining influence of the material base of a society. It has long since been abandoned by leading Marxist theorists. Indeed Engels later disavowed any connection with such views himself.[6] Nevertheless, economism represents an important theme in Marxist thought and it still exerts a considerable influence on Marxist interpretations of law.

The reasons for dissatisfaction with a crude materialist approach to law are threefold. In the first place there is no analysis of the relationship between law and other social institutions. All parts of the superstructure are characterized as direct reflections of the mode of production, so the relations between institutions of government and law, social relationships such as the family and the law, or moral and legal ideology are all ignored. This analysis is unsatisfactory because it fails to examine the close links between law and the state, and the possibility of interaction between moral values and the content of legal concepts and standards is apparently dismissed out of hand.

Second, an analysis of the functions of law is entirely absent. No reason is offered to explain why the law is needed to express the relations of production. In addition the role of the law in con-trolling relationships such as marriage which are outside the processes of production is beyond the horizon of an economistic perspective. Yet, in modern society at least, legal rules regulate many kinds of social arrangements beyond even the broadest conceptions of the relations of production. Thus statutes control the powers of institutions of government, placing limits on the discretion of the various administrative departments. By no stretch of the meaning of the material base of society could it be made to include such internal laws of the state apparatus. Similarly, modern legislation distributes rights within the family concerning marital status, ownership of property, and custody of children. It is implausible to suppose that such laws are performing functions directly related to the economic basis of the social formation. So the analysis of the functions of law must not only be rendered less opaque, but must also be investigated with regard to laws governing instances of social life removed from the material base.

Finally, and this is potentially the most serious defect in the crude materialist theory of law, the accounts of the fashion in which the material base determines the form and content of law remain crudely formulated. The idea that laws reflect existing patterns of social arrangements is an interesting and suggestive theory. Yet terms such as 'determines', 'expresses', or 'arises' tend to restate the problem of defining how the base influences the superstructure rather than providing an adequate solution to it. What is needed in order to transform these metaphors into a serious analysis of the origins of legal institutions and rules is a detailed explanation of the mechanisms by which social practices are transformed into legal systems. Marxists who view law from a crude materialist perspective have not succeeded in devising a clear view of these mechanisms. They have been content to make facile statements about the law expressing or reflecting the relations of production without conscientiously examining the process by which this occurs. At times their simple metaphors are effective in communicating the gist of historical materialism. For example, Pashukanis found it easy to point to close connections between practices of exchanging commodities under the capitalist mode of production and the developed law of contract found in modern legal systems.[7] It is evident that for the law to reflect such economic practices it must express certain assumptions which are shared by the participants. Thus the law governing the sale of goods must acknowledge the legal right to own private property and also the power to dispose of assets through a sale. These needs can only be satisfied by the law respecting the rights of legal persons to carry out these functions, whether they be acting as individuals or as members of a corporate group.[8] If the legal rules did not conform to this social framework and share these presuppositions behind the activity of exchanging commodities, then they would either be ignored or prevent the development of trade. Crude materialist theories of law thus aim to demonstrate that there are constraints of functional compatibility or correspondence between legal rules and modes of production. In this task they are moderately successful as long as their account is restricted to laws intimately bound up in the relations of production.

For the purpose of providing a materialist account of the bulk of laws in modern legal systems, it is unsatisfactory to rely on the simple idea of reflections of the material base. One reason is that it will often be impossible to point to any aspect of the relations of production which the legal rule is supposed to reflect. It can hardly be suggested, for example, that rules prohibiting rape or physical assault imitate some part of the production relations. There may, in fact, be a determining link between the material base and content of these laws, but the point is that the metaphors of reflection and expression are inadequate to provide a convincing description of that process. The deficiencies of the economistic approach become progressively graver as we shift our attention from customary legal rules to deliberate legislative acts. For example, a modern statute designed to penalize and deter the pollution of rivers is the product of considerable argument and debate motivated by groups who want to alter the practices of manufacturing industries. Such a law alters the relations of production to the extent that factories will have to make alternative production arrangements to avoid polluting activities. In what sense can this deliberate attempt to change a minor aspect of the relations of production be described as a reflection of that material base? Again, the metaphors of crude materialism prove to be unsatisfactory.

These defects in crude materialist interpretations of historical materialism are in fact only symptomatic of a deeper problem. What is lacking in the theory is an account of how conscious action is determined by the material base. In order to complete the crude materialist explanation it has to be demonstrated that individuals and groups are somehow constrained by their material circumstances so that they will only create laws which reflect the relations of production. This criticism applies equally to similar interpretations of historical materialism such as the one proposed by G. Cohen,[9] who argues that there is a functional relationship between law and the relations of production, just as there is a functional connection between the forces and relations of production. Here it is claimed that the only laws which are created are those compatible with the relations of production and promote them. Whatever the empirical merits of this claim, it is insufficient on its own, for it lacks a description of the mechanisms which control the actions of those persons responsible for enacting the laws in a society. How did it happen that in the early stages of capitalism a law of contract was developed which was suitable for a general system of commodity exchange? Why did those persons also create marriage laws which suited (if they did) the spread of the capitalist mode of production? The versions of Marxism closest to crude materialism require a more concrete description of the mechanisms by which the laws come to mirror or suit the material base.

In summary, the deficiencies of the economistic interpretation of Marx's theory of historical materialism are that it fails to examine the connections within the superstructure and to explain the functions of law as part of the superstructure; in addition, there remains the fundamental problem of devising a sophisticated theory of the mechanisms through which the base determines the superstructure. Although these criticisms may not necessarily be fatal to this version of historical materialism for it is possible that a complex version of economism could meet these objections, they are certainly very damaging, and helped to undermine the strength of this interpretation when it received a serious challenge from another strand of Marxist thought which emphasized the class character of the state and its legal system.

The second generation of Marxist thinkers at the turn of the twentieth century devoted considerable attention to political strategy. Their primary concern was to examine the nature of the liberal state and to define the appropriate attitude for European Marxists to adopt towards the system of power. The vital question was whether to participate in democratic elections. To do so would amount to a qualified endorsement of the bourgeois state, but to refuse to enter the democratic process seemed to leave Marxist groups out in the cold. Less radical movements appealed to the popular imagination by promising reforms without a wholesale disruption of the social order. Consequently in England where a social democratic party occupied a reformist position

Marxists were reduced to a small group of intellectuals. In order to avoid this political failure Marxists reconsidered their theories of the state and its legal system.

Taking their lead from Marx's and Engel's arguments in the Communist Manifesto that the modern state was an instrument of the ruling class for the suppression of the proletariat, these Marxists and in particular Lenin[10] added that the legal system was an integral part of the state with an identical function. Instead of laws being described as a reflection of the mode of production, they were explained as creations of the state apparatus to further the ends of the ruling class. The criminal law especially was a vital buttress supporting private ownership of the means of production on which the power of the ruling class rested. Rules prohibiting theft or physical assaults were thus explained not in the strained terminology of reflection as suggested by crude materialist interpretations of Marxism, but rather as direct expressions of the will of the dominant class.

In this instrumentalist analysis of law the connections established between the legal system and other social and political institutions are all related to the problem for Marxist theory of explaining social order in modern societies. Marx argued in the Communist Manifesto that historically all societies had been divided into antagonistic social classes. Although the concept of social class was not an original idea, Marx's criteria of definition were novel in social thought. Class was determined for Marx according to the position a person held in the relations of production. The most important division was created by access to the means of production. Those persons who controlled access to the means of production, whether it be land, natural resources, or a factory, were in a dominant position because they could use their power to secure political control over other social classes. The concept of class was therefore independent of conscious attitudes, levels of income, or behavioural characteristics. It depended strictly upon a position in the productive processes.

Marx reasoned that these social classes would necessarily have antagonistic interests. The owners of the means of production would seek to maintain their control and source of power, but the subordinate classes of peasants, serfs, and wage-labourers would resent their poverty and the restrictions upon their freedom. Any society would therefore be based upon social conflict. How then was social order maintained for the majority of the time?

The Marxist response was straightforward. In part threats of violence were a cause of stability, and occasions such as 'Peterloo' stood as a dire warning to any potentially rebellious subjects. The ostentatious use of force was rare, however, and so to explain social order entirely by reference to armed repression seemed to be unsatisfactory. The legal system was an obvious candidate for an additional mechanism of control. The criminal courts, prisons, and the scaffold or guillotine were hardly distinguishable from the use of brute force. It was easy to perceive law as a system of institutionalized violence. The legal system thus shared the task of class repression along with the other institutions of government including the armed forces, the police, and the bureaucracy.

This projection of law not only explained the law's functions and how it was linked to other political institutions but also provided an effective critique of traditional liberal political theories of law and the law's relationship to the problem of social order. For example, both Hobbes and Locke accepted the importance of the legal system for the maintenance of social order. However, they portrayed law as being similar to the rules of a game which prevent any one player from securing an unfair advantage. Marxists, on the other hand, insisted that law did not ensure a fair system, but on the contrary guaranteed the preservation of a particular mode of production and its corresponding class structure, thereby placing nearly all the available wealth and power in the hands of a fraction of the population.

Perhaps the chief strength of the instrumentalist analysis of law at a theoretical level lies in its response to the problem of consciousness and the relationship between base and superstructure. It provides a satisfying alternative to the elusive metaphors of economism. The origins of legal and political institutions are located in the pursuit of self-interest by a dominant social class. Laws are not reflections of the mode of production in any mechanical sense, but are deliberately constructed by the ruling class to serve their own interests. Of course, the rulers are not always free to pass any legislation which suits their fancy. According to the strength of resistance by subordinate groups, proposed laws have to be modified, or even held back. The link between base and superstructure is provided by the dominant class. The composition of that class is determined by the relations of production which have been established. That class then pursued their interests through the medium of political and legal institutions, the latter supplying a crucial coercive organization. In this fashion the class instrumentalist approach shows how the economic relations which determine the class structure of a society eventually exercise their influence on the law through the mediation of the state apparatus. In short, the economic base determines the legal superstructure, not instantaneously and mechanically, but through a process of class rule in which the participants further their interests through the legal system.

There are weak and strong versions of this class instrumentalist theory of law. In the weak version, not generally adopted by Marxists, it is pointed out that legal systems tend to preserve existing modes of production by favouring the established forms of ownership of property and preserving social order. Where one class holds most of the wealth, inevitably the law works to serve the interests of that class. The strong version emphasizes the instrumental quality of law. It is insisted that the state and the legal system are within the exclusive control of the dominant class, and that they deliberately use the law to pursue their own interests at the expense of the subordinate classes. The stronger version fits all kinds of law into the model of the ruling class imposing their will on the masses, whereas the weaker one allows for areas of law such as marriage which are of no direct concern to the ruling class and which can be affected by other interest groups.

Both versions agree, however, upon the coercive character of law. The principal function of the legal system is to repress those social classes which are excluded from wealth and power. Obviously criminal laws like theft which protect private ownership of property by threats of punishment are regarded as the paradigm of legal rules in modern society. Additional support for this coercive, instrumentalist concept of law is found in examples of unlawful government behaviour. When faced with serious popular rebellion a legal system will exhibit signs of strain by countenancing short cuts over legality in order to quell a revolt effectively. The fact that brute force has to be used if the criminal law fails to protect private ownership of property and a system of production is explained as proof of the function of law as a regularized and institutionalized tool of class repression.[11] Both the exercise of military force and the criminal justice system are directed towards a common goal with the former acting as a fail-safe mechanism for the latter.

The longevity and pervasiveness of the class instrumentalist theory of law within Marxism rest on the manner in which it provides solutions to the problems raised earlier with regard to the crude materialist interpretation of historical materialism. In the first place, it supplies a description of the links between different parts of the superstructure. The legal system is identified as a leading institution in the process of securing the interests of the ruling class, and it shares this role with the state and the military forces. It is the arm of the state apparatus which provides on a daily basis the standard institutional mechanism for the repression of the subordinate classes. Second, there is a clear view of the functions of law in terms of coercion to back up rules which serve the interests of the dominant class. Finally, and most important of all, the mechanism linking the material base with the legal superstructure is pinpointed. The determining force of the relations of production upon the conscious acts of legislation is provided theoretically by the concept of a social class. If it is historically true that the dominant social class, that is a group in a special position in the relations of production, has always pursued its interests by using the legal process instrumentally, then it follows that the material base does indirectly determine the content of law. Notice, however, that this solution is only available to the strong version of the class instrumentalist thesis, for only there is it held that all laws are motivated by the ruling class pursuing its own interests. The weak version requires an additional account of how laws which are not created by the dominant class are materially determined. Nevertheless, with the formulation of the strong thesis of how the base determines the superstructure, Marxism produced its first coherent theory of law which satisfied the principles of historical materialism.

(3) Objections to Class Instrumentalism

Although this conflict theory of society is still the most popular version of historical materialism, and with it the description of law as an instrument of class oppression remains a rarely challenged orthodoxy within Marxism, from its inception the conflict perspective has been subject to two criticisms which have become the focal points of discussion within modern Western Marxist writings. I shall outline these objections here, and then in the following chapters consider the Marxist responses to them in depth.

In the first place it must be doubted whether the class instrumentalist interpretation of law deals adequately with the problem of demonstrating the mechanisms of material determinism. The first scent of this trouble appears when we notice an ambiguity in the class instrumentalist theory. Is the claim of the class instrumentalist theory that all laws serve the best interests of the ruling class? Or is the claim merely that the ruling class pursue through law such ends as seem to them to be desirable? The former possibility indicates that the content of law must always coincide with their long-term interests viewed from the perspective afforded by the theory of historical materialism. The latter interpretation of the class instrumentalist theory allows for a divergence between subjective perceptions of interests and those interests defined by Marxism as vital for a ruling class to protect.

The principal difficulty with the former interpretation is that it requires the conscious behaviour of the ruling class always to coincide with their best material interests. Yet how does the ruling class manage to pursue such an undeviating course? Inadequacy of information and unsophisticated analysis, it might be supposed, might often lead a dominant group to forfeit important advantages or seriously endanger the mode of production on which its power rests. Indeed, this is probable, given the tendency of the dominant ideology in Western countries to reject Marxism in its entirety. This problem of demonstrating how the ruling class avoid legislating upon an erroneous perception of their interests becomes even more acute when they are credited with the skilful propagation of desirable beliefs and values through morality and religion. It is perhaps reasonable to suppose that the ruling class have a shrewd understanding of where their economic interests lie, but how can they be so sure-footed when favouring particular churches such as the Protestant or the Catholic, for example?

On the other hand, if it is admitted that the ruling class can deviate from the optimum path, and that their subjective perceptions of interest may conflict with their best interests as defined by Marxism, then a different kind of problem is encountered by the class instrumentalist theory. Presumably the claim that the content of law is determined by the ruling class requires that the bulk of the class share a common perception of their interests and goals. Unless the dominant class possess such a coherent viewpoint, then it is unlikely that their legislative aims will concide. The result would not be a legal system inspired by a clear vision of its purpose, but a loose collection of rules produced by the fluctuating forces of diverse political groups. Marx's definition of a social class, however, lacked this reference to solidarity of aims and methods. Membership of a class is determined according to a position in the relations of production, and it does not depend upon an individual's awareness of class relations or whether he identifies himself as a member of a particular class. Yet it is supposed by this alternative version of class instrumentalist theory that the ruling class move as one. So the theory assumes that the dominant class have a sense of group solidarity with commonly held perceptions of self-interest which are enacted in laws (even though these laws may not coincide with a Marxist definition of their best material interests).

In fact, there is a logical step missing whatever view is taken of the class instrumentalist theory of law. To support the thesis that all laws are instruments of class oppression, either there has to be an account of how motivations inevitably coincide with a person's objective class position, or it has to be explained how the social class becomes aware of itself as a group and comes to share a common perception of its interests. It is evident that to satisfy either requirement a more detailed investigation of the origins of ideologies and how they contribute to the creation of laws is necessary, for it is in the Marxist theory of ideology that the key to the material determination of perceptions of interest will be discovered. Such a theory would demonstrate how the material base conditions the form and content of consciousness, and leads to the formation of class-consciousness or perceptions of interest. In turn the process of the creation of law by conscious acts according to these determined perceptions of interest would be explained, The great strength of the conflict theory seemed to be at first sight that it replaced the weak materialist imagery of reflection with a more concrete analysis of the formation of consciousness and the motivations of people when making laws. With the recognition that the problem of explaining the material determination of perceptions of interests persists, that strength is shown to be illusory. Marxism still requires a sophisticated theory of the origins of consciousness within a materialist framework. Without it the phenomenon of law can never be adequately explained by the theory of historical materialism.

It can even be argued that the class instrumentalist theory represented a step backwards from crude materialism for the analysis of law. It has been suggested that the law is not only to be found in the superstructure as an instrument of class oppression, but also that it provides the rules by which the relations of production are constituted. In the society of hunters, for example, we identified the relations of production as the arrangements made for trapping the prey and distributing the food. Let us suppose that among the arrangements there is a conventional rule which requires every able-bodied man to participate in the hunt. The rule may be supported by such sanctions as ostracism, removal of privileges, or even expulsion from the community. Is this rule a part of the relations of production or is it superstructural in form?

From one perspective the rule is an essential part of the arrangements which constitute the relations of production. Without such a norm the success of the mode of provision of food supplies would be jeopardized by any small number of men unwilling to participate. The relations of production require a co-operative effort in order to perpetuate the community, so the rule appears to lie at the heart of the productive process, an essential ingredient of the relations or production. Yet from another viewpoint this social rule is closely analogous to law or morality which are located within the superstructure by the theory of historical materialism. The norm has arisen because of the exigencies of the mode of production and therefore appears as a superstructural phenomenon determined in its form and content by the material basis of the society. In practice it is hard to maintain the division between base and superstructure unless it is insisted that such rules are incorporated into the superstructure.

The problem of defining the relations of production becomes even more acute in a technologically advanced society. It seems impossible to conceive of the relations of production without resort to the basic legal framework of contracts and the protection of private ownership by the law of tort and criminal law. The crucial process of the extraction of surplus value from labour could not occur without a reliable framework of rules similar to the contract of employment. Again therefore there is the problem of defining the relations of production so that they do not include significant elements of the superstructure.

If this argument is correct, it wreaks havoc with the base and superstructure analysis. It is impossible to maintain that the material base determines the form and content of the legal superstructure when the material base is itself composed of law. In Chapter 4 I shall consider whether Marxists have provided adequate responses to this criticism of one of the core ideas of historical materialism. Before then, in Chapter 3, I shall look at the problem of consciousness in order to discover the Marxist explanation of how the ruling class know how to rule, and in particular how they use law as an instrument of class oppression. Through progressive refinement I hope to present a sophisticated version of the class instrumentalist theory of law which is at once internally coherent, consistent with the principles of historical materialism, and a persuasive account of the form and content of laws.

3. Ideology and Law

In the previous chapter I argued that for historical materialism to be theoretically coherent, it requires a convincing description of the process by which the goals and aspirations of individuals and groups are materially determined. The crucial defect of crude materialist and functionalist explanations of historical materialism is that the role of conscious action in historical events is left unexamined. These versions of Marxism assume that people conform to the mysterious constraints imposed by the material base without seriously refuting the contrary view that men are free to determine their own goals and act accordingly. In the context of the law a promising route towards the repair of this defect is provided by a version of class instrumentalism. It is argued that the ruling class, whose membership and interests are determined by the relations of production, use the state apparatus including the legal system to further their ends. This suggestion has the merit of trying to forge a link between the material base and the determination of political action. Yet there remains one objection against this defence of historical materialism. How, it is asked, do the ruling class become aware of their class interests and then act as one body in pursuit of them? In the first section of this chapter I shall eleborate upon the Marxist theory of ideology in order to demonstrate the plausibility of the contention that a common perception of self-interest emerges within the dominant class. For the remainder of the chapter I shall then consider the merits of such a claim when confronted with the variety of laws and legal systems.

(1) The Marxist Theory of Ideology

The first question concerning the origins of consciousness of class interest presents an epistemological issue: what are the origins of knowledge and insight? Marxists are often associated with two claims in this sphere. Some attribute to Marxism the assertion that all knowledge is false consciousness or at least that the present dominant conceptions of the world are false and only

Marxism has truly understood reality. We shall see that this is a major distortion of the mainstream of the Marxist tradition. A second claim associated with Marxism is one we have already encountered. The early Marxists who veered towards crude materialist forms of social explanation tended to use the metaphor of reflection to describe the relationship between the material base and conscious ideas. It was claimed that cultural achievements, scientific ideas, religious and legal thought were all merely reflections of the relations of production. This analysis is plainly inadequate, for in truth it leaves unexplained the process by which the material base is translated into conscious ideas. Yet once the metaphor of reflection is rejected, it proves hard to find a replacement which satisfies Marxists.

If we look to Marx's own writings for guidance, they are helpful in directing us towards the outlines of a Marxist theory of ideology, but it must be confessed that he never wrote a definitive text on the matter. The bulk of his work on the formation of consciousness consists of critiques of his contemporaries and mentors. They were hastily written when Marx was a young journalist, and most of them were only published posthumously. Nevertheless the tide of Marx's thought during his intellectual development is apparent. He found himself in the precarious position of waging war on two fronts. On the one hand he attacked the prevailing idealist tradition in Germany, and on the other hand he strove to avoid being taken over by the radical materialist forms of social explanation. Given the novelty and complexity of Marx's position, there was considerable confusion among his critics, and unfortunately, as we have already noted, some Marxists defected to the crude materialist camp. On the whole, however, Marxists have tried to steer their work in directions consistent with Marx's own middle ground. We can best appreciate this anlysis by looking at it in the context of the rival theories which Marx rejected.

The attack on idealism was an early undertaking. In notebooks and lengthy essays Marx grappled with the works of the dominant intellectual figure in Germany, the idealist philosopher Hegel. During this period Marx embraced the idealist notion that history has a goal, that patterns of progress towards an inevitable destiny can be discerned as one civilization succeeds another. Yet at the same time he rejected the idealist explanation of this process. Hegel's vision of history identified the sources of change and progress in the resolution of contradictory world-views, or interpretations of how society works together with evaluations of the political and social system. Marx was dissatisfied by the manner in which idealism suggested that these world-views and their syntheses were immanent in the human mind, waiting to be discovered by the exercise of reason and reflection upon experience. He introduced a modern style of sociological explanation of the origins of knowledge and consciousness by arguing that ideas were constructed through practical activities and social interaction as men conducted their daily lives. Marx summarized this view in his famous phrase, 'Social being . . . determines . . . consciousness.'[1] From this materialist perspective, ideas, knowledge, and motivation were neither arbitrary flights of the imagination nor the product of research into the recesses of the mind, but were constructed in response to practical experiences. It followed from the rejection of Hegel's idealist epistemology that Marx was unwilling to account for the evolution of society by a history of ideas. He believed that there had to be deeper sources of instability within the experiences of the historical actors which led them to branch out in new political directions.

Whilst conducting his polemic against idealism Marx tended to insist upon strong materialist interpretations of history. The central tenet of crude materialist epistemology is that the position of participants in the exploitation of natural resources determines what data they receive and what world views they form. Thus their ideas are reflections of productive activities, the relations of production, or perhaps more broadly of class relations. Although Marx accepted much of this materialist theory of consciousness, he developed two criticisms of it which together distinguish the Marxist tradition from simple forms of materialism.[2]

The first point concerned the notion that men were the passive recipients of ideas from an external world. Marx argued that this separation of men from matter with the only connection between them being the generation of ideas in response to material circumstances ignored the ability of men to transform their environment. There was , he asserted, a continuous interaction between consciousness and material circumstances in which deliberate action led to a change in material circumstance, and in turn this affected consciousness in the form of concepts, ideas and interpretations of the world. Thus an agricultural labourer's consciousness was not simply a reflection of his activities when working on the land. By his efforts the land was transformed into fields, paths, and waste. His activities would then give rise to further conceptions concerning the right to use the fields and roads and other broader ideologies. Thus in the theory of historical materialism the material world is not treated as a predetermined contingency but is understood as having been constructed by men and as being susceptible to further alteration as a result of conscious action.

Marx's second criticism of crude materialism was concerned with its epistemology. In the metaphor of reflection it was assumed that the sense data being received would automatically generate ideas. The concepts of field, harvest, and property ownership would emerge in the mind of the labourer simply as a consequence of working on the land. Materialism shared this view of the formation of consciousness with simple versions of empiricism. Marxism rejects this epistemology, and replaces it with the thesis that knowledge is formed through the ideological classification and comprehension of sense perceptions. The empiricist vision is of a naïve man receiving impressions from the world and then from these particular instances organizing his knowledge into patterns of understanding and insights into regularities. Marxists, elaborating on Marx, argue that on the contrary men must use ideological frameworks in order to interpret the material world. These ideologies act as grids for analysing experiences. They are acquired through all the processes of socialization including education and the mastering of linguistic skills. In practical activities these ideas are tested and examined, and this process may lead to refinement and then in turn to new social practices. So in the agricultural labour example the concept of a field would have been originally created during productive activities, but the concept was shared in a community because it was defined and explicated by an ideology present in that society.

The Marxist theory of ideology rests upon this combination of an epistemology which stresses the ideological nature of the acquisition of knowledge together with the way conscious ideas are formed by and help to shape the material world. The model fits together in the following complex schema. The set of signs and categories by which men interpret the world are formed originally in the process of socialization. Each person carries around an ideological grid acquired through education by which experience is translated into knowledge. In the course of men's productive activities, however, new ideas and values may be shaped in a continual interaction between thought and practice. These novel insights may be combined together to constitute an ideological grid to rival the traditional one. Eventually the pressure from contradictory ideologies may become so intense that a social, political, and intellectual revolution will occur.

The classic example of the emergence of contradictory ideologies is found in the origins of revolutionary consciousness. Marx argued that no revolution against the capitalist mode of production would occur until the proletariat had developed class consciousness and had demystified their bourgeois ideological framework. Only when they possessed the correct state of mind, amounting to a coherent ideology in opposition to bourgeois values, would they seize power by revolutionary action. How would this state of consciousness arise? Marx's answer pinpointed the importance of practices which could give rise to working-class solidarity. In trade unions and other labour organizations, where the awareness of class was heightened through daily conflicts with the owners of the means of production, counter-ideologies would be gradually formulated. Because factories brought workers together geographically and without differentiations in status, the working class would perceive itself as a class, positioned in a structure of class domination, and would then rise up against the system of exploitation. According to Marx the emergence of contradictory ideologies was the necessary precondition for all revolutions. There still lurks an element of the Hegelian dialectic of course in the notion of contradictory ideologies, but there is an important distinction as well. Marx makes it abundantly clear that the counter-ideologies of the subordinate class will only arise through certain kinds of practices. This is the nub of his theory of 'revolutionary praxis'.

Since Marx sketched out this theory of ideology, many Marxists have added refinements and qualifications; indeed my account benefits from their insights. Without adding further to the complexity of this account, it should be apparent that Marxism rests upon a theory of ideology which is quite distinct from that implied by the crude materialist metaphor of reflection. Furthermore, Marxists are not committed to the notion that all ideologies are false. On the contrary, since ideologies depend for their vitality upon interpretations of the material world, they must always in a sense be true for they incorporate plausible conceptions of reality. To be exact, the criteria of truth and falsehood are inappropriate once the empiricist epistemology has been rejected. All ideological interpretations of the world, including the natural sciences, are valid within their own scheme of things. The term false consciousness is used by Marxists narrowly to refer to the adoption of the dominant ideology by the subordinate classes. To the extent that this dominant ideology fails to match up to their experiences it is a misleading form of consciousness. It will also almost certainly function to legitimate the ruling class's hold on power by portraying the relations of production as the natural order of things. Clearly an essential element of revolutionary practice is to demystify such legitimating ideologies.

Armed with this Marxist theory of ideology it is possible to demonstrate the coherence of the class instrumentalist explanation of law. The problem identified at the beginning of this chapter was how to show that the material base determines the perceptions of interest held by the ruling class. If this link could be made plausible, it would then be possible to envisage a class instrumentalist theory of law. Earlier we noted an ambiguity in the class instrumentalist thesis. Did Marxists claim that every member of the class understood his best interests and acted accordingly? Or was it that the class shared a consensus view about their goals even if they might be mistaken about where their true interests lay? Both versions jostle with our sense of the contingent and arbitrary nature of human desires, and they also suppose a measure of consensus in the community which often appears to be lacking.

It is obvious that the class instrumentalist theory depends upon the second version. The ruling class share common perceptions of interest as a result of similar processes of socialization and experiences of productive activities. A consensus of values is established by the transmission of ideologies and their vindication through practical work. The other view of the class instrumentalist thesis could only be supported if a crude materialist theory of ideology were adopted. Then it would be possible to argue that everyone knows his best interests, for all ideas would be direct reflections of the material world. It is evident, however, that the Marxist divergence from crude materialism necessitates the interpretation of the class instrumentalist theory of law in which the dominant class tends to act as one because of the ideological basis of knowledge, even though the direction of their actions may not prove to be the most beneficial to their position.

In practical terms, what kind of analysis of law does this Marxist theory of ideology lead us to? The full implications of the theory of ideology are frequently missunderstood. It is assumed that Marxism endorses a simple conspiratorial interpretation of laws, in which the ruling class develops a view of its goals and then formulates laws accordingly. Some conception of the relative complexity of the Marxist position can be glimpsed by looking at an example which slips neatly into such a conspiratorial analysis. The English Combination Act 1800 was aimed at discouraging the spread of trade unions amongst wage-labourers. The statute endorsed and extended the existing law by declaring all trade unions to be criminal conspiracies. Obviously this legislation could be slotted comfortably into a conspiracy theory. It would be easy to argue that the entrepreneurial classes, having realized that trade unions threatened to reduce the profitability of manufacturing industry by demanding higher wages, used the law to deter workers from forming combinations. Yet this conspiratorial model would not be a Marxist explanation.

What Marxism seeks is the identification of practices upon which conceptions of interest and values are constructed. This will take place at many different levels, each having an impact upon the form and content of the law which is eventually produced. At one point a group may indeed emerge which constitutes a unified class, aware of its class position with clear perceptions of its interests in terms of its position in the relations of production. It may introduce legislation like the Combination Act. A Marxist will be particularly intrigued by such historical conjunctures because of their relevance to Marx's theory of revolution. He will search for the relations of production and practices within them which have given rise to that awareness of the structures of class domination. Mostly, however, class positions are only dimly perceived. Ordinary social practices and experiences are the breeding-ground for ideologies, which in turn determine the content of the laws.

In order to be certain what those practices were, and how the ideologies emerged, a detailed historical study would have to be undertaken. Here, only a few central themes will be described in order to provide the flavour of a Marxist approach. At the level of productive activities, the emerging form of the relations of production was an exchange of commodities or an employment relationship. These transactions took place between individuals who bargained for favourable terms. Out of this experience there arose an ideology which stressed the naturalness of an individualistic market economy. A free market ensured both efficiency and a fairness of transactions. Inevitably, the development of workers' combinations was perceived as a threat to the ideal of free individuals bargaining with each other in the market-place. Thus trade unions were understood within the dominant ideology as a form of illegitimate ganging-up by a group against a single person. Similarly, of course, combinations of manufacturers were regarded with suspicion, and were made illegal by the 1800 Act. The presence of such a section in the Act could not be persuasively accounted for by a conspiracy theory, for cartels could benefit entrepreneurs enormously. Only the complex Marxist approach to ideology can accomodate such a rule within its explanation of the content of the law.

On top of this basic assumption there were many other strands of the dominant ideology which supported an attack on trade unions. Practices involved in the enclosure movement and the decline of commons had led to a fierce belief in the sanctity of private ownership of land. Since political power and social status were also attached to property, the legal protection of family fortunes by equitable devices and extreme tolerance of landowners who injured trespassers were part and parcel of a general structure of domination. Any form of radical group challenged the stability of this political order, for reliance was placed rather more on threats to deter insurgents than on an ability to muster military force to crush dissidents. Fears for the preservation of private property in the political order were engendered by the French Revolution, and clearly any association of members of a subordinate class was worrying to landowners. So trade unions fell foul of a widespread hostility to any large grouping of persons which might be transformed into an unmanageable rabble.

Finally, it may have been the case that the entrepreneurial class were indeed aware of their class position in a Marxist sense, and realized what a challenge to the capitalist mode of production the unions posed.[3] But instead of that possibility being the centre of the Marxist analysis as it would be in a simple conspiracy approach, it is both unnecessary and tangential once the theory of ideology is properly understood. The sources of ideologies in productive activities past and present would provide the focus for an assessment of how the dominant class came to perceive legislation against combinations to be desirable.

Lest there should be any misunderstanding of this theory of ideology, it is worth pointing out that it is not asserted that every detail of ideologies is influenced directly by the relations of production. Only the broad outlines and the elementary themes of the dominant ideology are determined by social practices within the mode of production. There is scope for rival interpretations of those experiences. Furthermore their translation into legal concepts and rules may be handled by many permutations as a comparative study of the laws of industrial societies will reveal. Yet there should be a broad correspondence between the core doctrines of these legal systems because they share similar sets of relations of production.

Tying all these strands of the Marxist theory of ideology together, the central argument is that ideologies arise from and are conditioned by social practices in the relations of production. Since the class of owners of the means of production share similar experiences and perform approximately the same role in the relations of production, there emerges a dominant ideology which permeates their perceptions of interest. Laws are enacted pursuant to this ideology. Thus the Marxist theory of ideology has subtly transformed the claim about class oppression. Initially that claim indicated the presence of a conspiracy amongst an élite group who knew exactly where their best interests lay. There is no need, however, on the theory of ideology presented here to suggest that the ruling class is aware of its class position and deliberately sets out to crush opposition. Instead, its perceptions of interest will appear to be the natural order of things since they are confirmed by everyday experience. A corollary of this is that laws enacted according to the dictates of a dominant ideology will appear to the members of that society as rules designed to preserve the natural social and economic order. The ruling class will not have the oppression of other classes in mind, but simply the maintenance of social order.

On the assumption that the foregoing theory of ideology permits Marxists to establish a theoretically coherent interpretation of law, the next step is to test the thesis that law is an instrument of class oppression against our knowledge of legal phenomena. The remainder of the chapter will be devoted to such an empirical assessment of the Marxist theory of law.

Before we begin, we should be aware of the difficulties Marxists have experienced in approaching empirical work. To presume the objectivity and reliability of knowledge gained from personal experience would amount to a dismissal of the Marxist theory of ideology as soon as it has been developed. The whole point of the theory of ideology is to demonstrate the manner in which knowledge is acquired through ideological grids which provide our common-sense view of the world. If this is correct, then suddenly to embark upon a positivist empirical enquiry would involve Marxists in a contradiction. This tension emerges vividly if we suppose for a moment that it is a current theme of the dominant ideology to emphasize the independence of law from class control. How can we hope to achieve a satisfactory empirical assessment of the Marxist theory of law when our shared ideological perceptions of the world are founded upon a contention which expressly denies the validity of the thesis that law is an instrument of class oppression?

On the other hand, if Marxism is to defend its claim to be scientific, some attempt must be made to test the theory against reality. It is not an exaggeration to say that the dilemma faced by Marxists between the pursuit of positivist empiricism and a subtle appreciation of the ideological acquisition of knowledge has led to enormous rifts within the Marxist tradition. Empirically-minded historians such as E. P. Thompson have slated the aridity of the theoretical schemes of philosophers like Althusser. In response, it is argued that mere empiricism is an erroneous methodology given the way Marxists believe that knowledge is acquired; a preliminary task of demystification of current ideological conceptions of the world is necessary for any serious Marxist understanding of history.[5] Each side in the debate has a fair point, and I can foresee no satisfactory reconciliation of their positions. Here I shall try to avoid both extremes, and whilst using empirical evidence to defend the Marxist theory of law, at the same time I shall endeavour to be sensitive to the need for circumspection when using my common-sense understanding of the world.

The method of my assessment of the Marxist theory of law is not so much by way of illustration of the thesis as by way of offering defences against standard kinds of objections. I have divided the criticisms into two sections. In the former, a conflict view of social formations is accepted. In other words, it is common ground between Marxism and its critics that any society is composed of conflicting groups, and that law is mixed up in the business of preserving social order. Critics object, however, to the description of the conflict in terms of social classes, arguing, instead, that a large variety of groups pursue their interests by attempting to affect the political and legal institutions and rules of the society. A second group of opponents to the Marxist theory of law deny that law is the product of conflict between groups. They assert that law is not so much an instrument for achieving certain ends, but rather an embodiment of justice and right which transcends mundane considerations of material interest. I shall consider the second kind of objection in section 3.

(2) Class Reductionism

Like all social theories which identify systemic relations within social formations, Marxism encounters the criticism that it is reductionist. According to the critics of reductionism societies are composed of independent units, the relations between them being undetermined and contingent upon how individuals have chosen to construct them. It is claimed that inevitably the Marxist emphasis upon a material base and dependent superstructure presupposes a degree of co-ordination and homogeneity which is lacking in social formations. Therefore it is alleged that Marxism tends to suffer from the dangerous vice of reductionism which is to misconstrue the diversity of social phenomena in order to confirm the rigid systemic framework of historical materialism.

It is precisely this charge which has been laid at the door of the class instrumentalist theory of law. It is alleged that the Marxism, inspired by its sophisticated notion of the material determination of perceptions of interest, forces all aspects of the legal system into a closely determined framework in which law furthers the interests of the ruling class by an oppressive network of institutions. This simple analysis of law encounters the criticism that social formations, including their legal systems, have a greater degree of complexity than such a reductionist explanation can hope to grasp. Attempts to substantiate and illustrate the Marxist thesis have thus been dismissed on the ground that in order to fit all laws into the pattern of class instrumentalism, Marxists have indulged in the vice of reductionism.

One standard objection in this vein focuses on the Welfare State. It is frequently pointed out that many laws in modern society indisputably favour the interests of the working class and cannot be characterized as instruments of class domination. In addition to social welfare legislation such as social security payments and health services, legally recognized political rights like universal suffrage are held up as examples of this phenomenon. The weak version of class instrumentalism may be correct to hold that in a general sense law contributes to social order and therefore it protects the interests of the wealthy and powerful against those groups wishing to displace them. But in particular instances the strong version of class instrumentalism fails because some laws benefit subordinate classes too.

A second criticism of Marxist reductionism accepts that laws are the product of class struggle, but rejects the concept of class advanced by Marxism. It is argued that, instead of the composition of a social class being determined by a position in the relations of production, all kinds of groups can form classes provided they develop a sufficient sense of solidarity to become politically effective. The strength of this criticism of Marxism derives from empirical evidence and, in particular, it finds support in Marx's own writings. In his masterpiece, 'Capital', Marx examined the origins of the Factory Act 1844,[6] a piece of English legislation designed to control the hours of work of women and impose severer restrictions upon the use of child labour. A simple class-interest analysis would suggest that this Act was a great victory for the working class for it ameliorated their conditions of work. Yet Marx's explanation is considerably more complex. Although he acknowledges the importance of the working-class Chartist movement in forcing such legislation through Parliament, he also indicates three other factors at work causing smaller groups to support the passing of the Act. First, manufacturers who had conformed to the spirit of earlier laws on the same subject wanted protection from competitors who were successfully avoiding the controls on child labour, so they supported a tightening up of the laws to close loopholes, thus preventing further undercutting of prices through the use of cheap labour. At the same time, according to Marx, manufacturers generally wanted a political alliance with the working class in industry in order to force a repeal of the Corn Laws. A final group supporting the Factory Act was the landlords, who were feeling the squeeze on the level of rents as a result of the progressive impoverishment of the working class. Whether or not these insights into the motivation of groups are historically accurate, the whole analysis demonstrates Marx's own rejection of simple class-based descriptions of the origins and functions of laws.

Of these two objections to class reductionism, I shall argue that only the latter presents a serious challenge to the Marxist theory of law as developed here. Nevertheless both can be accommodated within a more sophisticated analysis than any so far ventured above. I shall consider the two types of criticism in turn, paying special attention to the modifications and refinements which they force upon the class instrumentalist theory of law.

Relative Autonomy

In response to the argument that modern legislation often favours subordinate classes, Marxists provide two layers of defences of the class instrumentalist theory of law. In the first place, there is no reason why Marxists should deny that subordinate classes have an effect upon the content and enforcement of legal rules. Given a division of society into conflicting social classes, it is inevitable that the working class will resist certain repressive pieces of legislation. Yet such negative reactions to particular laws would not account for the phenomenon of welfare legislation where the working class manipulates the law for its own ends. Therefore, second, Marxists acknowledge that the dominant class does not have exclusive control over the state apparatus in modern society. It is possible for subordinate classes to make real gains by securing beneficial legislation. Nevertheless, Marxists maintain that such gains are minor, and only marginally detract from the background control over the State exercised by the dominant class.

Looking in more detail at the first layer of defence of the class instrumentalist theory of law, we should notice that here the emphasis is upon law in its application. In theory, the dominant class may be able to pass fierce oppressive laws, but in practice either it will desist because such laws will create social divisions and class conflict unnecessarily, or it will refrain from fully implementing a tough legal code in the face of popular resistance. In a remarkable study of law and order in eighteenth-century England, Douglas Hay reveals the series of subtle mechanisms by which the full rigours of a harsh penal code against property offences were adjusted according to local political factors.[7] This process of political accommodation in the application of law may be achieved by formal procedures in the legal system such as the prerogative of mercy, or it may be infiltrated as an unarticulated consideration guiding the exercise of discretionary powers such as decisions made by prosecutors on whether or not to pursue a case. Indubitably juries in criminal trials serve a similar function, permitting divergence from the legal norms when they conflict with popular conceptions of justice.

In general Marxists stress the degree to which the class struggle affects the implementation of law. Subordinate classes can put up passive resistance to laws or even organize campaigns of avoidance and disobedience as was the case with the English Industrial Relations Act 1971. On the other side, the dominant class will also seek to neutralize the effect of welfare legislation by persistent litigation and even systematic breaches of the law as in the case of the early Factory Acts. We can describe this phenomenon of class struggle in the application of laws by the term 'the limits of the law'. Marxists recognise that the dominant class is constrained in the kinds of laws which it can hope to enforce because of the strength of resistence from subordinate classes. There are no theoretical restrictions upon the content of law, but political conditions impose severe practical limitations.

Yet, as we have noted, the phenomenon of the limits of the law cannot explain how the subordinate classes have managed to adopt law as an instrument to turn against the dominant class by enacting welfare legislation. Does this negate the claim that law is an instrument of class oppression?

Marxists accept that the modern State including its legal system is notable for its considerable degree of independence from the control of the dominant class. The owners of the means of production do not overtly manipulate the politicians in democratic societies, but permit a degree of struggle within the state itself. Compared to earlier social formations the absence of personal control by the dominant class is remarkable. Yet Marxists deny that the State is completely autonomous, claiming that ultimately the dominant class determines the direction of political initiatives and ensures that the legal system serves to perpetuate the mode of production. The democratic process disguises the presence of class domination behind the mask of formal equality of access to power. Marxists refer to these peculiarities of the modern State by the concept of relative autonomy.[8] This term incorporates two ideas: first, that there is in reality less direct manipulation of political power by the dominant class in modern society than there was in earlier social formations, and, second, that the appearance of autonomy conceals deep structural constraints upon the powers of the State apparatus which ensure that it faithfully pursues the interests of the ruling class.

The potential utility of the concept of the relative autonomy of the State is obvious. It permits a Marxist to brush aside instances of working-class success in legislation, for these laws can be accounted for as merely examples of the relatively autonomous State at work. Of course, Marxism must demonstrate positively how the deep structural constraints arise to delimit the activities of the State. But if this can be achieved, then the basic theme of the class instrumentalist theory of law is preserved, albeit with some qualification. In the final chapter I shall consider the reasons for the relative autonomy of the State in capitalist social formations. For the present we must confine the discussion to an exploration of the mechanisms by which the dominant class controls the exercise of State power.

The most obvious method by which owners of the means of production indirectly control State action is by using power derived from ownership of capital. Any serious proposals to alter the capitalist mode of production will be met by a removal of support from an economy. Capital can be transferred from one country to another through the medium of multinational corporations. The ensuing crisis of unemployment and the declining value of money will put pressure on a government to return to the course of preserving the essential aspects of the capitalist mode of production. In the light of these constraints upon political reform, welfare legislation is regarded by Marxists as only a marginal incursion into the framework of capitalism. Nationalization of certain industries can also be seen not as a move towards the socialization of the means of production, but as a measure to help the remaining private sector of the economy by providing cheap sources of energy and transport.

Behind these economic constraints upon political action there lie deeper factors which delimit activity. Marxists emphasize the importance of the dominant ideology in setting the bounds of acceptable political action. The ruling class uses its position to disseminate its own world-views and values throughout a society. If it is successful in the propagation of the dominant ideology then everyone's common-sense ideas about right and wrong, rational and irrational choices, and even aesthetic judgments, will be formed by the assimilation of ideas supplied by agents of the ruling class. The pervasiveness of this ideological hegemony will prevent the development of alternative political perspectives within the working class, and thus ensure that the autonomy of the State remains within the bounds required by the capitalist mode of production.

The work of Gramsci[9] and Althusser[10] has been of prime importance in bringing ideology to the forefront in the Marxist analysis of the structural constraints placed upon a modern State. They argue that many social institutions play a part in ensuring the construction of beliefs and values which are in accordance with the dominant ideology. The education of children in schools is permeated by bourgeois values. Thus history is taught so that modern liberal democracies are the acme of the evolution of human societies. Similarly, churches teach deference to authority and property ownership. The mass media either provide escape from the real circumstances of life by emphasizing sport and scandal, or provide information which systematically ignores the class structure and the presence of exploitation. According to Gramsci the working class is bombarded throughout its life with propaganda containing the ideology of the ruling class.

The legal system plays a vital role here. In particular the legal framework of rules and doctrines provides a comprehensive interpretation and evaluation of social relationships and events which is in tune with the main themes in the dominant ideology. Because the legal system is encountered frequently in daily life, its systematic articulation and dissemination of a dominant ideology are some of the chief mechanisms for the establishment of ideological hegemony. Modern criminal codes, for instance, express theories of responsibility for actions which are individualistic and rest upon a belief in the presence of free choice whenever a deviant act is committed. Thus close attention is paid to the state of mind of the accused at the moment of the performance of the proscribed act in order to assess whether he was aware of the risk he was running. Only certain kinds of pressures which are primarily composed of threats of physical violence are considered to remove the accused's freedom of choice. Yet under different theories of responsibiltiy, economic pressures and fear of homelessness or starvation might be sufficient to provide defences to a criminal charge. What legal texts and judges achieve by repeatedly expounding the criminal law is that the particular ideology of responsibility found therein infiltrates the consciousness of all social classes, thereby constituting their common-sense view of justice. Consequently, everyone is genuinely shocked by the judge who refuses to convict a woman for theft because she is starving, even though on reflection members of the subordinate classes might see merits in the decision.

Similarly in the context of legal reforms which constitute part of the welfare state, working-class initiatives are founded upon bourgeois conceptions of rights. Their claims imitate established political values, and hence new laws serve to inculcate instruction in the dominant ideology. For example, many countries have laws which allow courts to test the fairness of managerial decisions to dismiss an employee. These laws are predicated upon an assumption of the natural right of the owners of capital to determine security of employment, and whilst they may constrain this freedom, they inevitably acknowledge the basic right. Thus an essential theme of bourgeois ideology is articulated by the law even whilst it is being slightly qualified.

It must be admitted that this ideological determination of the activities of a relatively autonomous State is difficult to prove and even hard to perceive amongst the chaotic rivalry of competing visions of social justice offered in modern societies. Nevertheless ideology plays an enormously important role in the Marxist account of the modern State, and if it is a valid analysis, then the existence of laws which favour the working class tends to confirm the category of relative autonomy rather than to defeat the class instrumentalist theory of law. The State, therefore, has scope for political struggle and independent action, but only within broad guidelines determined by the owners of the means of production and the dominant ideology. The laws of the welfare state remind Marxists of the important ideological functions performed by the law, but do not undermine the whole of the class instrumentalist theory. Provided it is understood that a special feature of the modern State is its ability to admit legislation which is beneficial to the working class whilst at the same time remaining incapable of supporting any serious challenges to the mode of production, then Marxists may retain their broad claim that law serves the interests of the dominant class albeit not always exclusively or directly.

Intra-class Conflict and Survivals

A second criticism of the class instrumentalist theory of law was put forward at the beginning of this section in connection with the Factory Act 1844. The question was how does Marxism account for laws which are enacted as a result of pressure from groups and associations other than social classes? This question forms part of a more general attack upon the Marxist tendency towards class reductionism. It is common ground here that societies are composed of conflicting interest groups and that laws are enacted according to the balance of forces among them. Critics of Marxism insist, however, that the composition of these groups cannot be satisfactorily explained in terms of social classes. Instead, if we look closely at all the groups pushing and tugging in the legislative mêlée, we find instances of intra-class conflict between for example landlords and manufacturers, contests between ethnic groups, and regional rivalries. So the criticism of class reductionism is not simply that some notable Marxists, including Marx himself, were unfaithful to their own premises, but more fundamentally that the source of conflict in a society cannot be persuasively explained by reference to social classes alone.

A closely related problem for the class instrumentalist theory of law is created by survivals.[11] Marxists have often acknowledged that legal rules may still exist even though they were first established under a former mode of production. Thus some feudal notions of property rights may be current in English law long after the capitalist mode of production has become dominant. A plausible way of accounting for such persistence is to suggest that a group which is separate from the ruling class has successfully used its influence to preserve the law. The legal profession is frequently accused of maintaining obsolete technicalities and of mystifying the law by expressing itself in esoteric language in order to protect the livelihoods of its practitioners from do-it-yourself lawyering. Whether or not this is a conscious process on the part of lawyers, it could have the effect of generating survivals which hamper the ruling class in its methods of exploitation. The English system of conveyancing may be a case in point. Although registration of title and the simplification of rights over land would serve to eliminate the need for expensive legal procedures when buying and selling real property, the procedure remains complicated because lawyers resist any movements for change with considerable tenacity. Here then we find lawyers, a group other than a social class defined according to classic Marxist principles, causing a law to survive even though its effects are contrary to the interests of the dominant class. As in cases of intra-class conflict, the reductionist implications of the class instrumentalist theory of law are rebuffed by empirical examples of survivals.

It is, however, easy to exaggerate the frequency of the occurrence of survivals. We must be careful to distinguish the form of words constituting the legal rule from their meaning when applied to particular circumstances. The same legal concepts may still be in use, but that does not prove the existence of a survival, for the words may now be interpreted differently. Thus, although English lawyers speak in the feudal language of property tenure when referring to ownership of land, as for example calling ordinary ownership 'freehold' thereby signifying that the land is held free from feudal incidents of tenure, owners of real property may rest assured that this continuity of language conceals major substantive reorientations of the law towards the absolute ownership required by the capitalist mode of production. Karl Renner argued in his book *The Institutions of Private Law and their Social Functions*[12] that similar instances demonstrated that a legal norm could remain constant whilst its social function altered. As his example he took the basic rule in Austrian law concerning ownership of property. This law expressed in abstract terms the principle that the owner had exclusive rights of possession and enjoyment over the land. The effect of this norm in a mode of production composed of independent peasants and craftsmen was that the worker would receive the produce of his own labour since he owned the means of production. The same general rule, however, ensures that the capitalist who owns the means of production becomes entitled to the products of the labour of his employees. Renner asserts that the legal norm is identical but its social function has changed from one of rewarding labour to that of licensing exploitation. In fact, only in a trivial sense has the rule endured whilst its social function has changed. The words or symbols used to express the rules have remained constant, but their meaning has surely altered since they are being applied in novel contexts. For Renner's thesis to be significant, it must be supposed that a rule can have a meaning independent of its effects on social behaviour.

There are three further reasons for being suspicious about the existence of survivals. First, if a statute continues long after the class which propagated it has been removed from a dominant position of power, it may not constitute a survival because it is simply ignored. This happened to the action for breach of promise of marriage in England. Such a claim for damages was predicated on a view of marriage which emphasized the dimension of property transfer rather than personal sentiment, a focus appropriate to the world of Jane Austen but anachronistic by the time of Mr Pickwick. But no reform occurred until 1970 because actions had largely died out.[13] The dominant ideology had inhibited the bringing of such claims even though the laws remained on the books. Second, the law may perhaps be easily evaded and so survive because of its irrelevance. The Bubble Act 1720, for example, prevented the use of joint stock companies in England even though they were needed by the beginning of the nineteenth century to hold accumulated capital. Yet the Act does not amount to an anomalous survival of aristocratic power because the simplicity of an alternative legal mechanism found in the law of partnership allowed the interests of mercantile groups to be fully satisfied; the Bubble Act lingered on because it was at the most a minor inconvenience.[14] Finally, an apparent survival which seems to run contrary to the interests of the ruling class may have been surreptitiously put to a new use. Thus laws prohibiting movement of labourers into towns were originally designed to preserve order in the countryside and limit the importance of the boroughs during the decay of feudalism. Later on they could be used by the bourgeoisie to quash rebellions by urban mobs, for merely by their presence in a town the wage-labourers were committing an offence. It was therefore extremely useful to keep these laws on the books and to rely upon selective enforcement to ensure their compatibility with the goals of the dominant class. Far from being survivals, these laws became instruments of social control in the hands of the new ruling class.[15]

Therefore the number of survivals in a legal system may be overstated, but undubitably some laws persist despite their inconvenience for the dominant class. A common Marxist explanation of the persistence of anachronistic laws is found in the support given to them by minor social groups such as lawyers. There is an essential similarity therefore between the problem of survivals, instances of intra-class conflict, and the multiplicity of group alliances behind social legislation like the Factory Act 1844. All of these laws seem to be created as a result of conflicts between groups which cannot be identified in class terms. Can Marxism admit such a possibility and simultaneously retain the class instrumentalist theory of law?

There is a clear danger in any acknowledgment of the role of groups other than social classes in the creation of law. The strength of the Marxist determinist thesis rests upon the link forged between the material base and the motivations of the principal actors in a society. As long as the relevant groups are social classes then this materialist connection is theoretically sound. Ideologies are formed in productive activities. The dominant class shares the same position in the relations of production and acquires a similar set of beliefs and values which are then relied upon to shape the political and legal superstructure. Once it is admitted, however, that laws are the product of conflicts between a host of interested groups united by factors other than their class position then the thesis of material determinism is gravely weakened if not lost altogether. There is nothing left to tie the actions of those groups to ideologies formed in the relations of production.

Some interesting attempts to rescue the class instrumentalist theory of the state and law from this objection distinguish between major class divisions and minor fractions within social classes. A fraction of a class is defined by Poulantzas as a group which has achieved a degree of autonomy from the rest of the class and has the potential of becoming a class itself.[16] The Factory Act 1844 might be explained as the product of an alliance between the working class and various combinations of class fractions such as landlords. With the aid of this carefully formulated class analysis, which avoids the pitfalls of a simplistic dichotomy of owners of the means of production and the proletariat, we may reinterpret laws as the product of conflicts between classes or potential classes which at the time only form a group within the dominant class. When analysing social phenomena in this vein there is always a danger that Marxism will degenerate into a general conflict perspective which has lost touch with material determinism, but at least a more subtle approach to the delimitation of the boundaries and connections between social classes may enable a Marxist to explain a wide range of laws in a manner consistent with the principles of historical materialism.

Nevertheless I doubt whether such a programme can be entirely successful. In order to explain the Factory Act 1844 or survivals, Marxists are constrained to bring into the account groups such as lawyers and manufacturers who have conformed to the spirit of earlier laws, neither of which groups can be identified solely by reference to its position in the relations of production. The legal profession provides just one instance of an independent group concerned with its unique interests which continuously affects the form and content of laws. As we investigate each legal rule we discover that different combinations of groups have sought alliances with each other in order to influence the direction of the law. Indeed, the membership of the groups is constituted as much by the features of the particular dispute as it is the inevitable product of conflicts of interest between classes and class fractions. The kaleidoscope of group alliances resists a class instrumentalist interpretation of their origins. Unless a route can be discerned for joining the class instrumentalist theory of law to a broader instrumentalist approach encompassing many groups within the confines of the materialist explanation of ideology, then the Marxist theory of law can only be maintained by indulging in all the vices of reductionism.

One possible response is to limit the claims of Marxism to manageable proportions. Instead of seeking to provide an analysis of all social phenomena including law, Marxists can argue that historical materialism only applies to the broad outlines of social evolution. The significance of the material base on this view is that transitions from one mode of production to another plot the course of history towards a Communist society, but the productive activities cannot be used to explain particular historical events. There is a theoretical difficulty, of course, in separating general patterns of social evolution from isolated occurrences, for those patterns can only emerge when evidenced by particular events.

Assuming, however, that Marxism could support its claims by reference to broad historical movements, then the dissatisfaction felt with class reductionism would be avoided. But the cost would be immense. It would no longer be appropriate to study the details of history, politics, culture, sociology, or law from a Marxist perspective for there could be little to say except to point to the presence of one dominant mode of production and to predict its eventual downfall. The cutting edge of the analysis of social phenomena in class terms and the dominant ideology would thus disappear. Needless to say few Marxists have ever accepted such a restrictive interpretation of historical materialism when all around them they perceive political struggles with a class character. The essence of Marxism is its explanation of the method for discovering the correct revolutionary practice, and this requires an understanding of the precise nature of the social formation. Anything less than a detailed social explanation would therefore be inadequate.

Faced with the unpalatable choice of so limiting the claims of historical materialism Marxists prefer to circumnavigate the objections to class reductionism based upon the multiplicity of the sources of social conflict by insisting that however diverse the groups may appear, and no matter how disadvantageous to the ruling class a survival may be, all can be explained by an awareness of the plasticity and omnipresence of the dominant ideology. The perceptions of interest held by the ruling class can be inflated to cover matters of no immediate importance to their position. Thus, their support through law for the established church or familial responsibilities can be accounted for by extensions of ideologies which are pertinent to practices in the relations of production. The church teaches deference to authority and private property, which could be useful to an owner of the means of production seeking to discipline his work-force. Similarly, familial ties such as paternal control over the marriages of his offspring could be linked to dominant ideologies concerning ownership and disposition of property. Furthermore the pervasiveness of the ideology of the dominant class should not be underestimated. We have already noted how bourgeois ideology is inculcated into the masses through such institutions as schools, churches, the media, and the courts. So the apparent variety of interest groups conceals, according to Marxists, an underlying unity of perceptions and values steered by the ideologies of the dominant class. Consequently the content of the laws will in the main be compatible with that ideology. The subordinate classes and class fractions will seldom affect the content of the legal rules to the serious disadvantage of the ruling class, for they have a double hurdle to overcome. Not only must they win a political struggle to capture control of the legislative organs, but also they must free their perceptions of interest from contamination by the pervasive dominant ideology of the ruling class.

The same argument applies to groups which cannot be defined as class fractions. Lawyers, for example, like other members of the community are imbued with the dominant ideology. Indeed they are especially prone to indoctrination because the legal rules they learn so precisely express the world-views and values associated with the dominant class. Those survivals for which lawyers are responsible will therefore rarely depart from norms indicated by the dominant ideology. On this defence of class reductionism therefore, laws not apparently linked to the class struggle are in fact inspired by a plastic and omnipresent ideology formulated by the ruling class as a crucial element in the defence of their dominant position.

More generally, the existence of survivals can be explained in two cumulative ways. First, they may occur as a result of a particular legitimating ideology used by the ruling class in modern society. Respect for laws can be enhanced by mystifying their function as instruments of class oppression. One way to obscure this purpose of law is to insist upon law's traditional origins and stable content. Its source in tradition tends to negate the claim that the law is an instrument of a modern ruling class, and the immutability of legal rules suggests a connection with basic conceptions of justice rather than the contingent interests of the ruling class. The success of this tactic of legitimation will be impaired if the law is changed frequently according to articulated goals. This was one reason behind the considerable opposition to codification movements in the United States during the nineteenth century, for excessive use of legislation undermines the authority of law by revealing its instrumental quality.[17] It follows that the endurance of survivals can be explained as instances where the ruling class is insufficiently inconvenienced to reform the law, given a general disposition to preserve the stability of the legal system.

The emphasis upon tradition suggests a second reason for the existence of survivals. Although, according to Marxism, the principal source of the dominant ideology is derived from practices in the contemporary relations of production, to the extent that law adheres to earlier ideologies because of the importance of traditional legitimation, there is bound to be an enormous mixture of ideologies represented in the law at any one time. These contrasts are not only found in a disjuncture between the words expressing the rule and the effects of the rule on social practices as we noticed in the English system of conveyancing. They go to the root of the arguments available in the relevant legal doctrines. Fundamental antinomies between legal principles based upon past and present relations of production can be revealed in even trivial matters.

Some of the resulting complexity of the task of deciphering the origins of ideologies behind particular legal decisions can be glimpsed in a contractual dispute taken from the English common law. In *Sagar* v. *Ridehalgh & Sons Ltd.* [1931] 1 Ch. 310 (C.A.) an employee claimed that certain sums of money representing his wages were owed to him. In their defence his employers explained that it had been their practice to make deductions from pay for bad workmanship by the weavers in their cotton mill. Counsel for the defendants submitted that this custom had become a term of Mr Sagar's contract of employment, so the deductions had been made lawfully. The Court of Appeal accepted this argument and the plaintiff's case was dismissed.

The court was faced with a choice between two rules. On the one hand the management argued that it was fair to impose standards of quality. They relied upon the customary practices of the industry to support this norm of behaviour. These customs both represented and endorsed a traditional view of the employment relationship formulated in pre-capitalist eras.[18] At that time the employer was master, and the worker a mere servant. The master was entitled to use a wide range of disciplinary measures such as deductions from pay in order to maintain productivity and order in the household. On the other hand, the employee relied upon the doctrine of freedom of contract. This is a basic principle of contract law derived from a theme of individual liberty in bourgeois ideology corresponding to the productive activities of commodity exchange under the capitalist mode of production. Mr Sagar argued that only those terms which he had agreed to accept at the formation of his contract were binding upon him, for to slip in additions by operation of law was to flaunt the basic principle of freedom of contract. Here then was a contradiction between ideologies: the traditional disciplinary powers of management against the principles of freedom of contract. Notice that it was the employee who was relying upon the dominant ideology whilst the employers rested their case upon older conceptions of the employment relationship. The employee was constrained by legal rules which incorporated the dominant ideology from offering an alternative vision of the position of a wage-labourer. At the same time the employers were able to find legal rules and precedents to defend the lawfulness of their behaviour.

The court's solution embodied a compromise. It was held that the employer could make the deductions only if the right to do so had become a term of the contract. As a result of the customary practices over a number of years, however, the term would be implied into the contract on the basis of a well established but narrow exception to the principle of freedom of contract which permitted the introduction of terms provided they were based upon well-known and reasonable customs. Now, to understand the complexity of the ideological basis of this one case it is necessary to consider both pre-capitalist and capitalist modes of production. No simple equation can be found to link the modern dominant ideology with the content of law. The tangled web of legal doctrines can conceal anachronistic survivals as well as permitting subtle metamorphoses of the existing legal doctrines.

In sum, the class instrumentalist theory of law can defend itself against criticism of Marxism's tendency towards class reduction-ism provided that the pervasiveness of the dominant ideology is recognized. Marxists explain the existence of laws which benefit subordinate classes as part of the phenomenon of the relative autonomy of the modern state. Such legislation will never challenge the fundamentals of the capitalist mode of production because of the control exercised by the dominant ideology over all reformist movements. Similarly, conflicts between groups other than social classes are fought out within the terrain of the dominant ideology. Occasionally there will be ambiguities and contradictions in that ideology which will have to be sorted out in the political process and through litigation. Particular groups may seek to preserve earlier ideologies, and so legal survivals may persist. On the whole, however, my argument is that Marxists may defend the class instrumentalist theory of law against the allegation of class reductionism by relying upon the determining force of the dominant ideology.

(3) The Autonomy of Legal Thought

I turn now to another kind of challenge to the class instrumentalist theory of law. Here the criticisms are more fundamental, for they go to the root of the instrumentalist conception of the functions of law. In contrast to the previous section, objections are raised against the portrayal of law as an institutional arrangement by which conflict between ideologies and interests can be resolved. Law is perceived rather as the cement which glues together a social formation on the basis of agreed principles of right conduct. Law is equated with justice, not the imposition of a dominant ideology. Thus the emphasis is upon a consensus of values in the explanation of social order, and those ideals are regarded as supra-historical and undetermined by material factors.

A belief in the autonomy of legal reasoning is shared by lawyers and citizens in most legal systems. In extreme cases all valid laws are said to be derived from an exercise of reason by those responsible for devising the legal codes. This is true of societies whose legal systems are based on sacred texts. The prophets and priesthood elaborate the principles of law to be discovered from the basic tenets of right conduct embraced by the religion. In Islam the writings of the Koran have served for centuries as the source of the sacred laws called the Sharia. Similarly, the Hindu laws (*dharmasastra*) were fixed through the authentic interpretations of sacred revelations by a caste of holy men. A belief that all laws are the product of reasoning is not confined to rules associated with religions. Traditionally the concept of natural law has been limited to the presence of a divine cause, but versions of the underlying idea can be purely secular. In this latter form, the natural law school adopts a teleological view of nature in which all things including mankind have an intrinsic purpose or function. Beginning with the conjectured purposes of human society, these philosophers devise through the exercise of reason appropriate definitions of right conduct for men. On these extreme views, law is an approximation to a transcendental reasoned collection of principles of correct behaviour, far removed from the pragmatic solution of mundane conflicts of everyday life. Law is the embodiment of right: the rules are either divinely inspired or created using reason to discover objectively valid principles which accord with natural justice.

A more circumspect opinion is to be found in modern jurisprudence. It is admitted that legislatures usually alter the law deliberately to satisfy certain interests. There is, however, a degree of mystery to law. In the development of legal doctrine, a special kind of reasoning takes place which is irreducible to the interplay of conflicting interests, the elaboration of the dominant ideology, or the forms of political argument.[19] Although there is considerable disagreement about the exact nature of legal reasoning, especially over the degree to which it even departs from straightforward instrumentalist concerns, some common ground exists. It is accepted that legal discourse, at least on its surface, operates according to standards of coherence and consistency which differentiate legal reasoning from debates about material interest.[20] Those like Dworkin[21] who believe that the surface appearance of legal reasoning corresponds to the actual process taking place, argue further that lawyers are not at bottom concerned with instrumental policy considerations, for there is a kind of legal logic which provides solutions to disputes independent of perceptions of interest held by lawyers, judges, social classes, or any other group. Proponents of the full autonomy thesis further argue that this method of reasoning towards the just solution to disputes is carried out in an independent sphere of rationality in which the results are not determined by the background dominant ideology. They view legal reasoning as a discrete and non-instrumental articulation of investigations into justice.

The form and location of this dialogue vary among legal systems. In entirely codified legal systems such as that in France, the dynamic of legal doctrine derives from the opportunities to be creative provided by the ambiguities of the meaning of the words composing the rules. Lawyers can exploit the vagueness of the written law to deal with new problems and to effect subtle transformations in the content of the laws. Other legal systems such as those of Great Britain and the United States of America do not rely entirely upon the authoritative texts of statutes for the sources of law. They are supplemented by the rules of Common Law. If there is no legislation on a topic, in order to reach a decision a court must first establish what rules and principles are entailed by the precedent decisions before applying those standards to the case in hand. So in the Common Law during the formulation of the rule as well as in its interpretation opportunities arise for judicial creativity. For the sake of convenience I shall concentrate on judicial reasoning in Common Law countries but my remarks are intended to cover other occupational groups who use legal reasoning.

At the outset we should distinguish the thesis of the autonomy of legal thought from the concept of relative autonomy. In the first place, the idea of relative autonomy refers to the institutional framework of the capitalist state and its freedom from direct control from the dominant class. The autonomy of reasoning on the other hand does not presuppose or refer to a particular institutional framework; it may arise both in capitalist and in pre-capitalist legal systems such as Roman law. Indeed, as we shall see, it is less widely accepted in modern society. Second, the thesis of autonomy suggests a complete independence of legal thought from all material constraints, whereas the whole point of the concept of relative autonomy is to insist that despite the institutional isolation of the modern state, underneath it is as much within the power of the ruling class as any other form of government. At base, the thesis of autonomy is an idealist conception which runs contrary to the Marxist theory of ideologies.

There is, however, one link between relative autonomy and the thesis of autonomy. Where the job of articulating and developing laws is handled by a distinct caste of lawyers, who are not identical in their composition to the ruling class, it is much easier to suppose that they reason without concern for the material interests of the dominant class, and furthermore that not all their ideas are derived from the dominant ideology. In a relatively autonomous state therefore it may be more widely believed that law develops autonomously because the officials of the legal system are not obviously manipulated by the owners of the means of production.

A crude instrumentalist analysis of legal thought is often attributed to Marxists. This instrumentalist view is diametrically opposed to the thesis of autonomy. It holds that the formalism of legal reasoning is a sham. Behind the beguiling vision of autonomous juristic logic, there lurk the sinister machinations of class rule. Judges manipulate the law to suit the interests of the dominant class, but they hide their activities beneath legalistic rhetoric. Although this instrumentalist view of legal reasoning is associated with Marxists, it is hard to find writers who both adopt it and claim to be Marxists. Furthermore there are both empirical and theoretical reasons why Marxists should avoid associating themselves with crude instrumentalism.

The first objection is simply that the thesis of autonomy provides a more accurate description of legal reasoning. This can be illustrated by a judicial decision taken from English criminal law. In *R. v. Miller*, [1954] 2 Q.B. 282, a woman had deserted her husband and had begun divorce proceedings. At this time Mr Miller had sexual intercourse with her against her will, leaving her in a hysterical and nervous condition. He was charged with rape and assault. At the Winchester Assizes, a criminal court of first instance, the judge found that there was no established law governing a charge of rape in such circumstances. Most lawyers had always assumed that a man could not be convicted of the rape of his wife, but there was neither clear legislation nor precedent decision to that effect. Lynsky J. consulted numerous authorities in order to reach a decision. He relied upon remarks made by highly esteemed judges in earlier cases, like "Stephen J., one of the greatest authorities on criminal law" (in *R. v. Clarence* (1888) 22 Q.B.D. 23). In addition the works of learned authors on treatises on the criminal law were studied with great care.

The law on this matter was first dealt with many years ago in Hale's Pleas of the Crown. There it is said that 'a husband cannot be guilty of rape upon his wife for by their mutual matrimonial consent and contract the wife hath given up herself in this kind to her husband which she cannot retract' (1 Hale P.C.629). . . . One can well imagine that, in the days when that book was written by Sir Mathew Hale, that was the accepted view of the law because at that time a valid marriage could not be dissolved except by death, and the only way in which a marriage could be avoided was by Private Act of Parliament.

There is no hint in the judgment of instrumental considerations being taken into account, either of a class nature or for the protection of the interests of differently constituted groups. On the contrary, the judge diligently searched for a consistent view about the appropriate rule among the authorities without mentioning consequentialist considerations. He treated the mass of legal doctrine as a giant jigsaw puzzle which had to be fitted together to form a coherent picture. Occasionally a piece does not fit, the rules do seem irreconcilable, but the subleties of juristic logic eventually point to a distinction which resolves the contradiction and an unbroken scenario emerges. Here the conflict lay between a general prohibition against rape and the institution of marriage which not only permits sexual intercourse but requires it between husband and wife for the union to be legally valid. This was reflected in opposing pronouncements on the matter by judges and learned writers. Lynsky J. reconciled these rules by holding that a man may have sexual intercourse with his wife whether or not she consents without infringing the prohibition on rape unless and until a court has made an order which separates the spouses. As no such separation order had been issued, the husband retained an immunity from prosecution for rape, though in one of those characteristic ironies of the criminal law he was promptly found guilty of assault.

We may not wish to condone this judgment on the ground that it takes an unrealistic view of the nature of the consent given to sexual intercourse by a woman during a ceremony of marriage. On the other hand one could respond that the decision protects a husband from false accusations of rape which might undermine the stability of marriage and waste the time of the courts. Yet whatever view one takes of the justice of the result, it is hard to believe that judicial reasoning is entirely instrumental. Lynsky J. sought a solution from a rationalization of conflicting authoritative pronouncements. A synthesis was achieved by examining the basic principles of the law and weighing them against each other. The categorical statements of Hale and Stephen were weakened, and an exception to the traditional view of lawyers introduced through reliance upon more recent opinions. Such considerations as the encouragement of marriage or the reduction of violent crime were not mentioned and apparently played no part in the reasoning. The whole matter was dealt with in the same fashion as priests examining holy texts in order to discover the meaning of right concealed therein. It is this pursuit of coherence which both supports a belief in the autonomy of law and refutes any purely instrumentalist explanation of legal reasoning. In particular, the typical instrumentalist picture of judges scheming to suppress the working class by new twists of legal doctrine seems a grossly distorted image of the serious endeavours of judges to gather a body of law into a seamless web.

If legal reasoning were truly instrumental we might expect to see jagged edges where laws conflict and issue contradictory instructions. Each rule would be the product of the balance of conflicting forces, manufactured in the vicissitudes of class struggle.

As the political weight of each class increased or diminished, the laws would be affected, leaving the promulgated rules as an unstable, inconsistent morass. The experience of lawyers confutes such a quagmire, though certainly the consistency of the law can be exaggerated. There are creases in the fabric of the law which have to be ironed out as in Miller's case, but over-all a modern legal system presents its student with a challenging body of closely reasoned doctrines more thorough and sophisticated than most other forms of normative discourse.

Furthermore, the appearance of this method of reasoning gives support to the other aspect of the autonomy thesis, namely that juristic logic escapes the constraints of the dominant ideology. The judge takes pains to restrict his train of thought to the internal logic of the legal system. He seeks to place his decision in established typologies and under hallowed principles. He avoids appeals to broader values and legitimating ideologies. This suggests that legal reasoning operates autonomously, undetermined by the dominant ideology.

Thus the autonomy thesis seems to provide a better description of the process of legal reasoning than simple instrumentalism. This first objection is countered by the crude instrumentalist approach. It is argued that we must distinguish appearance from reality, and that the judicial endeavours to secure coherence and consistency are only a sham which conceals their active preference for the interests of the ruling class. But why should we believe that there is this huge gap between appearance and reality? The answer given by crude instrumentalist theorists is that the whole nature of the legal system as an instrument of class oppression is obscured if laws are thought to have been created independently of material considerations. This distortion must serve as a useful legitimating ideology for the structures of power. Furthermore, lawyers conceal their own power by pretending that the law develops independently of their own concerns.

To a certain extent this argument is valid. There may be a considerable divergence between the factors a judge actually takes into account and the standards voiced in his opinion. Typically, personal experiences and politically sensitive consequentialist considerations will be excised from a judgment, even though they may have weighed heavily in the assessment of the merits of the case. Nevertheless, to disbelieve in the process of legal reasoning completely requires a great degree of cynicism. It has to be supposed that all those lawyers who participate in doctrinal disputation are either enjoying the game of perpetrating a conspiracy on a grand scale or they are suffering from an enormous delusion.

Equally significant from our point of view is a theoretical objection to this instrumentalist interpretation of legal reasoning which argues that this interpretation diverges from the Marxist account of ideologies. We saw above that Marxism does not account for the motivations of the ruling class by reference to their understanding of their material position. Instead, their ideological perceptions of interests originate in material practices and socialization. The dominant ideology represents common sense understanding of the world and elementary principles of morality. It is this ideology which directs the judicial sense of justice, and provides it with a sense of the relative weight of conflicting arguments. The ideology has considerable plasticity and provides opportunity for diversity of thought within the ruling class. It is not equivalent to a narrow set of conceptions about material interests, as the class instrumentalist theory of legal reasoning suggests. Indeed, it may lead in directions which are contrary to objective class interests. Thus, not only does instrumentalism rest on an erroneous claim about the fictitious nature of legal reasoning, but also it is in danger of losing touch with Marxist principles of social explanation.

Rather than summarily dismissing the experience of legal reasoning as an illusion, an increasing body of Marxists are incorporating the autonomy of legal reasoning within their interpretation of law. Engels was probably the first Marxist to admit that the subtle rationalizations of legal discourse belie any instrumentalist explanation. In a famous letter to Conrad Schmidt he argued that codes of law were not unmitigated expressions of self-interest proclaimed by the ruling class.[22] Instead, the pursuit of interest was often balanced by the constraints of maintaining a consistent conception of right; the law had to be coherent and avoid self-contradiction. Indeed Engels goes further than simply distancing himself from any form of instrumentalism, for he concedes that legal rules escape the determining effect of the material base. He introduces a version of the thesis of the autonomy of law in which some legal rules are the product of non-instrumental and discrete modes of discourse. Other writers have followed this lead,[23] hotly castigating instrumentalism and insisting that law has a degree of autonomy. It is hard to be sure what is meant by this claim. The concept of autonomy (and sometimes, confusingly, relative autonomy)[24] is used in contrast to crude instrumentalism without receiving a careful definition. The claim could mean that legal reasoning is the product of the dominant ideology (as opposed to a direct reflection of the material base) which would be in tune with the Marxist approach outlined in the previous section. Often, however, the term autonomy is used to imply that legal thought escapes material constraints entirely, as if legal ideology were like a kite when the string is let go.[25]

Marxists should be wary of adding their weight to the slogan that law is autonomous. In joining this bandwagon they risk a departure from the principles of historical materialism. To accept the reality of autonomous legal reasoning is to flirt with a general attack on any kind of social theory which involves material determinism. Marxism is committed to a systemic theory of social explanation which emphasizes the determining control of the relations of production on all aspects of the political, legal, and cultural superstructure. Although those Marxists who accept the partial autonomy of legal reasoning have not been explicit in their descriptions of juridic logic, what seems to be suggested is that the fundamental principles of law are materially determined, but within these constraints legal reasoning selects solutions to particular concrete problems. In other words, the dominant ideology produces the basic standards of justice, the underlying categories and values of the legal system, but through a logical process judges articulate the precise implications of these norms. According to this view, in Miller's case we must presume that the basic laws governing marriage and rape were materially determined, though their reconciliation in the judgment depended upon juristic logic.

The question arises, however, of what prevents the judges from altering the basic principles through legal reasoning? Indeed, it is difficult to imagine how this could be avoided. If the basic principles purport to order the rules of a legal system into a coherent body of doctrine, then when legal rules are produced by independent logic, this may occasionally force adjustments in the fundamental principles. Legal reasoning may corrupt the original standards of the legal system through a continuous dialectic between the particular rules and their generalized rationalizations. If this can happen then the content of law will move progressively further away from principles determined by the material base until the connection is merely historical rather than presently effective. For instance, the result in Miller's case requires the basic principles of the laws of marriage to be reconsidered in order to accommodate a limitation of the husband's sexual privileges. This may introduce a circular process of adjustment between fundamental principle and individuated rules until the laws of marriage are entirely transformed by juristic logic, without any material determining force to account for the change.

To accept the autonomy of legal reasoning, therefore, is to run the risk of abandoning any illuminating materialist explanation of the content of law. Furthermore, it poses a threat to the materialist explanation of all other aspects of the superstructure, for if the content of law develops autonomously then may it not affect the social practices which it governs? If legal doctrine requires new kinds of behaviour, the law will be generating social change independently of material influence. The legal superstructure will be acting as an autonomous agent affecting social practices without there being a determining influence from the material base.

The implications for history and social theory of acknowledging the autonomy of law are thus unexpectedly immense. Their significance can best be illustrated in the context of the controversy over the relationship between law and the rise of capitalism. It has seemed natural to Max Weber and many others[26] to suppose that the capitalist mode of production must rest upon a reliable system of the law of contract. Indeed, the existence of a law of contracts to govern commodity exchanges appears to them to be a prerequisite rather than an effect of the growth of the capitalist mode of production. Weber reasoned that businessmen needed highly predictable results to flow from their commercial transactions if they were to risk their capital in new enterprises. Thus the law of contract had to be clear in its effects and reliable in its methods of enforcement. What was unique to Europe, and thereforecould help to explain why capitalism flourished there first, was the tradition of Roman Law with its sophisticated doctrines designed to solve contractual issues. The ancient texts provided the intellectual heritage necessary for European lawyers to forge the required law of contract in time for the take-off of the industrial revolution. This explanation of the origins of capitalism of course depends upon a belief in the autonomy of legal reasoning. The doctrines of contract had to precede the emergence of the capitalist mode of production, and lawyers had to reason their way towards those rules without receiving an impetus from bourgeois ideology. I have sketched this issue extremely crudely here, but the central point about the challenge to historical materialism posed by the thesis of the autonomy of legal reasoning is thereby highlighted. If the independence of the development of the legal superstructure is conceded, then the base and super-structure analysis is undermined. The Marxist belief in the deter-mining effect of the relations of production upon the remainder of a social formation gives way to the idealist view that law may evolve autonomously and then cause changes in society. Historical materialism cannot admit the existence of free-floating ideologies affecting the course of events without gravely endangering its fundamental principles concerning the material determination of social evolution.

Thus Marxists find themselves in an uncomfortable predic-ament. If they stick to a purely instrumental explanation of legal reasoning, which is at best a dubious interpretation of the principles of historical materialism, then the whole enterprise of ensuring coherence and consistency in legal reasoning has to be dismissed as false consciousness, perpetrated by lawyers who are concerned to mystify their desire to support the interests of the ruling class. On the other hand, an acceptance of the autonomy thesis poses a threat to the whole theory of historical materialism. Marxists will never be able to extricate themselves from this predicament as long as they accept the terms of the debate in which they are engaging. At present both camps confine themselves to an inquiry into how the judge or jurist is cogitating. The question is whether a judge follows instrumental considerations with a class character, or operates a discrete mode of reasoning.

But to pose the issue in this way is almost to concede the point to idealist explanations before argument has commenced, for if attention is limited to the judge, it is already implied that legal reasoning is a purely intellectual exercise taking place entirely in the mind of the individual. From there it is a short step to an acceptance of the autonomy of legal reasoning from material influences. Recall, however, the principal contention in the Marxist theory of ideology: social being determines consciousness. Marx insisted that ideas and values were produced as responses to activity rather than being present in the brain waiting to be discovered or revealed. This theory of ideology should apply equally to legal doctrine. As part of the cultural superstructure, legal thought must be permeated by the dominant ideology. Legal rules articulate and reconcile the perceptions of interest and the value-systems emanating from different classes and class fractions within the productive activities. All these points have been axiomatic to the theory of law put forward here. It follows surely that to direct attention away from social practice and the formation of the dominant ideology to the individual's mind alone at this late stage is inconsistent. What we should be looking for are the sources of the reasons given for the development of legal doctrines. A Marxist should expect to find them in the dominant ideology and the social practices on which it is based.

Of course, to insist that legal doctrine is merely a particular kind of expression of the dominant ideology is not to deny the possibility of divergences, inconsistencies, gaps, and changes. The origin of the ideology in social practice permits individuals to express the variety of their experiences in diverse ideas and values, though the ideological basis of the acquisition of knowledge ensures general conformity to the dominant ideology. Therefore there is always scope for different interpretations of a set of production relations, and this allows countries with similar material bases to have diverse dominant ideologies, which in turn leads to a variety of legal conceptualizations of similar problems. Furthermore, disagreement may arise about the proper formulation of the legal articulation of the dominant ideology within one legal system. Thus the claim that legal doctrine is essentially an expression of a background ideology does not entail the consequence that laws of countries should be expressed in the same way, nor that there cannot be genuine disagreements about the content of the rules within a single legal system. Also it should be remembered that the dominant ideology is neither static nor unchallenged. Conflicting interpretations of the dominant ideology may signify that a period of transformation is being experienced. Lawyers may be able to support conflicting claims by the use of earlier and later ideologies. We saw above, in *Sagar* v. *Ridelhalgh & Sons,* a case where an employer relied upon pre-capitalist ideologies and their legal expression whilst the employee took bourgeois individualistic ideology at its face value and insisted that the new doctrines of freedom of contract be applied to him in their entirety.

Obviously in many instances it will be difficult to disentangle the precise origins of legal doctrine and demonstrate the source of the conflict between legal rules. We can glimpse this complexity in Miller's case. What were the sources of ideological conflict present in that dispute? In feudal and early modern times rape was regarded as an interference with the rights of the husband or father, and like other offences against public order and property, deserving not only of an award of compensation (not of course to the woman) but also the calumny of public disgrace at a criminal trial. From such a perspective it followed naturally that a man could not be charged with rape of his wife for that would be analogous to charging someone with the theft of their own property. The advent of capitalism had dramatic effects upon the dominant ideology concerning the legal status of individuals. We have already noted how commodity exchange relations presuppose a measure of equivalence in legal abilities to own property and make contracts. This clearly had an impact on legal personality as a whole and in particular affected ideological perceptions of women's status. Instead of being treated merely as men's appurtenances, they have been increasingly recognized as completely equal and separate persons. Inevitably this change in legal status had ramifications for the relationship of marriage, and Miller's case represents just one instance of this reorientation of the dominant ideology having effects upon legal doctrine.

The picture of doctrinal development sketched here departs considerably from typical versions of the thesis of the autonomy of legal reasoning. There is no imaginative jurist or wise judge thinking out elaborate intellectual systems of justice, but rather doctrinal evolution occurs when a conflict arises which cannot be dealt with straightforwardly because it raises to the surface an internal contradiction within the dominant ideology. Hard cases are therefore not crises of inconsistency thrown up by the logical development of the existing law; they occur when no legal expression of the dominant ideology has been established or during periods of ideological transition when there are competing background ideologies. Ultimately the material determination of the content of law in these hard cases is ensured because the dominant ideology is itself the source of the conflict between legal rules; it defines the issues to be discussed and delimits the range of possible solutions. What can never be accepted by a Marxist is the view that each legal rule is not the product of a dialogue with the background ideology. A grip is never lost on the kite string, even though it may flutter about in the winds of change.

It should be evident that this explanation of legal reasoning runs contrary to the crude instrumentalism often erroneously associated with Marxism. Instead of lawyers and judges serving as the lackies of the dominant class by furthering its material interests wherever possible, doctrinal development is portrayed as an anxious search for rules which correspond to common-sense ideas of right and wrong based upon the dominant ideology. We can accept the reality of the qualities of consistency and coherence in legal reasoning, but our understanding of those phenomena no longer coincides with that of the thesis of the autonomy of law. Those aspects of legal thought do not signify that lawyers are operating a discrete mode of discourse with its own system of values and logic. Lawyers are concerned with coherence and consistency because they are attempting to resolve conflicting interpretations of the dominant ideology, and their solution must be persuasive if it is to command the respect necessary for the perpetuation of that ideology. The form of this discussion is admittedly one of reconciling legal rules, but those rules are only perceived to be in conflict and a solution is only reached by reference to the standards provided by the dominant ideology. Thus for a Marxist, during the evolution of legal systems, the life of the law has been in neither logic, nor the search for ultimate truths about moral values, nor the imaginative ability of lawyers and judges to manipulate their learning to suit their masters, but in the need to resolve contradictions within the dominant ideology which force themselves upon the consciousness of jurists in the guise of conflicts between legal rules.

It may be asked why the symbiotic relationship between law and the dominant ideology is not more widely perceived? The answer here harks back to the earlier discussion of survivals. In so far as the authority of a legal system rests upon traditional legitimation, there will be a tendency to limit legal discourse to discussion of established rules. If every innovation has to be based on existing rules or principles, then obviously broad-ranging discussions of justice and reasonableness will be eschewed. Legal reasoning will, therefore, appear to be discrete as long as lawyers are obliged to frame their arguments on authoritative traditional sources of law. Behind this appearance of a discrete mode of discourse, however, the dominant ideology will be at work providing both the cause of the uncertainty and the parameters of acceptable results.

There is a further and deeper reason why legal reasoning so often appears to be autonomous. Many social formations have contained political structures which have rested their claims to legitimacy upon compliance with law. This is true of both a religious autarchy and a modern liberal state. The former government ensures that it upholds the sacred laws, whilst the latter makes its prime virtue obedience to the Rule of Law. In such societies where law is equated with justice or legitimate authority, the thesis of autonomy plays a vital role. Where doctrinal evolution is masked by obsessive concern for compliance with the letter of the law, the aim of upholding the law appears straightforward and uncontroversial. Lawyers reason in a manner which reinforces the idea that doctrinal development is discrete and non-instrumental. They are formalistic in their approach, favouring repetitious articulation of the established rules over careful assessments of rival interpretations of existing doctrine. The thesis of autonomy is connected, therefore, to particular kinds of political legitimation, and it both affects and is confirmed by legal practices. We shall tackle this form of legitimating ideology from a Marxist perspective in the final chapter. For the time being, the conclusion we have reached is simply that the features of legal reasoning associated with the thesis of autonomy can be explained by the principles of historical materialism, and that the class instrumentalist theory of law in a sophisticated form can emerge from our discussion unscathed.

(4) Critique of Ideological Hegemony

So far in this chapter we have looked at the relation between law and ideology in Marxist theory, and have rebutted a number of objections to it. We concluded that the material determination of the content of law occurs through the medium of the dominant ideology. This connection ensures both that subordinate classes and other groups are unable to affect the laws significantly, and that the legal superstructure can never escape the gravitational forces of the material base despite the apparent autonomy of legal thought. Although this defence of class reductionism with its emphasis upon the ideological hegemony of the dominant class is extremely common among Marxists, I find it ultimately uncon-vincing, so I shall briefly note my reasons for dissatisfaction.

One reason for this is the elusiveness of the theory when it is tested against empirical evidence. Because the dominant ideology is said to be plastic and omnipresent, it is possible to eliminate any counter-examples without difficulty. Laws which do not obviously fit into the pattern of class instrumentalism are accounted for as ramifications of core ideologies supported by the ruling class. The contrary suggestion that some legal rules cannot be explained on a class basis at all, for example that laws prohibiting rape and assault further the interests of other kinds of groups or perhaps benefit everyone equally, is often casually dismissed as naïve or the product of false consciousness.[27] It is said that the dominant ideology portrays such laws as universally valuable in order to legitimate their authority, while in fact they form part of the general state apparatus for the oppression of the subordinate classes. Here then we find that the Marxist theory of ideological hegemony undermines our attempts to be scientific in the testing of claims of historical materialism against the evidence before us. It seems that no satisfactory route can lead us out of this swamp.

There is a further, and even more disturbing aspect of the version of the class instrumentalist theory of law which relies heavily upon the ideological hegemony of the ruling class. Let us look more closely at the claim that the dominant ideology is plastic and omnipresent. What is the source of the elasticity of the ideas and values and are there any limitations upon their malleability? Surely this is a disguised form of conspiracy theory in which the ruling class supports such institutions and values as happen to seem to it to be a good idea? There are no boundaries to the tractability of the dominant ideology provided that any new directions appear to serve the interests of the ruling class.

My earlier objection to conspiracy theories was that they were unfaithful to the Marxist explanation of ideologies. The problem arises because conspiracy theories fail to situate ideologies in material practices. Instead of ideas and values emerging from interpretations of productive activities, conspiracy theories tend to suggest that members of the ruling class and their acolytes develop ideologies in an instrumental fashion according to the direction which best suits them. Instead of attempting to account for the ideology of political equality in the nature of the practices involved in the capitalist mode of production, conspiracy theories suppose that the idea of equality is dreamt up by political philosophers as a legitimating device which confirms the moral authority of the bourgeois state. As a result the coherence of the Marxist theory of ideology is lost, because the link between the material world and ideologies disappears. It seems as if ideas and values are developed independently of experience of practical activities, and the only link between cultural phenomena and the material base is that the dominant ideologies will always be chosen to serve the interests of the ruling class.

We saw precisely this process of extrapolation in the analysis of the ideological basis for Miller's case. From the fairly plausible contention that a system of commodity exchange induces an individualistic ideology in which everyone has certain equivalent legal rights to own property and sell it, we jump to the vague ideas of equal protection of the law, the recognition of women as independent from their male protectors, new conceptions of sex roles, the function of marriage, and so forth. As these ramifications become more and more distended, the explanation depends less upon generation of ideologies in material practices than upon deliberate manipulation which smacks of conspiracy, not material determination.

Yet the alternatives to the class instrumentalist theory of law remain equally unpromising. If a serious attempt is made to situate the ideologies behind all legal rules in productive activities, large areas of the law are left unexplicated. As we noted in relation to the crude materialist theories of ideology, it is plausible to link some of the doctrines of the law of contract to the practices of commodity exchange. But as our attention shifts to legal rules which govern subject matter only remotely connected to productive activities, it becomes progressively more difficult to provide a Marxist account of the ideologies behind the laws.

Marxists therefore find themselves in a dilemma. If the principles of the Marxist explanation of ideologies are strictly adhered to, large gaps in the account of laws appear. If, on the other hand, the plasticity of the dominant ideology is stressed, there seems to be a break with the original structural style of explanation of ideologies for the crucial link between the relations of production and the ideological superstructure appears to be broken and replaced by a crude form of conspiratorial instrumentalism.

4. Base and Superstructure

(1) Law in the Material Base

In the previous chapter my aim was to defend an interpretation of historical materialism which relied upon the base and super-structure configuration. I have argued that the essential Marxist insight is that we must look to the relations of production in order to understand a society's structures of power, the origins of its culture, and the sources of instability and change. The kernel of the analysis of law thus lies in the determining effect of the material base upon the legal superstructure. For this theoretical framework to be successful, two essential steps in the argument must be defended. First, we must differentiate clearly between the material base and all aspects of the superstructure. If we should fail to disentangle the political, legal, and cultural aspects of a society from its relations of production, then Marxism would lapse into incoherence. Second, the mechanisms by which the material base determines the form and content of the super-structure have to be explained. We must establish the link between productive activities and the vast range of political, legal, and cultural phenomena, for otherwise the principal insight of historical materialism would be lost. The previous chapter was devoted exclusively to the second contention. Because of the difficulty and centrality of Marx's concept of ideological determination, that discussion merited our attention first. Yet the investigation of the mechanisms of material determinism could only take place on the assumption that the first contention could be proved, namely that it is possible to distinguish the relations of production from the superstructure.

In recent years this contention has been attacked by critics of Marxism, and Marxists have noticeably tempered their enthusiasm for the base and superstructure model.[1] We glimpsed the reason for this turnabout at the end of Chapter 2 during our examination of the hunter-gatherer community. We noticed that some rules, such as the requirement for able-bodied men to participate in the hunt, went to the root of the relations of production. Without that rule the mode of production would be prone to disaster. Although at first sight the rule was a super-structural phenomenon akin to law or morality when we looked closely it appeared to be a part of the relations of production as well.

Plamenatz has pressed home this criticism of the distinction between base and superstructure in the context of later modes of production.[2] He points out that the manner in which Marxists describe different modes of production is in the terminology of legal rights and duties concerning ownership and exchange. Thus feudalism is understood by reference to the legal obligations arising from tenure of property, and capitalism is distinguishable because of the absence of incidents attached to private ownership of the means of production. Not only are the relations of production described in legal terminology, but Plamenatz further argues that modes of production are constituted by the power relations established by the legal system. Ownership is composed of rights to prevent others from forcibly taking property or interfering with it; without legal norms and sanctions provided by a legal system, there can be no such thing as ownership, merely possession maintained by personal force. If private ownership of the means of production is the hallmark of capitalism, then Plamenatz concludes that those relations of production are dependent upon a legal system. Obviously this conclusion undermines the distinction between base and superstructure. So Plamenatz contends that it is impossible for a set of relations of production to be described without reference to legal rules, and furthermore that many modes of production like capitalism are actually dependent upon the legal system for the creation of their basic economic relations.

In addition to these criticisms, a more general point can be made against any description of the material base which excludes a normative element. Modern sociology emphasizes the part played by rules in the formation of stable relations involving a measure of reciprocity.[3] These rules provide a framework within which men interact; they define roles and expectations and provide conventions as the basis for communication and co-operation. Furthermore, rules supply reasons for action and standards by which others may be criticized. All of these functions of rules are necessary for an adequate conception of the relations of production. Only if the arrangements for production are governed by norms could they be sufficiently stable and reliable for a regular pattern of social institutions to arise upon them. This is particularly evident in modes of production which rely upon commodity exchanges. The normative framework of a law of contract or its equivalent is necessary for the participants to engage in commerce. Without the existence of remedies to protect a contracting party, it is unlikely that many complex transactions with their attendant risks would be undertaken. When Marxists refer to participants in particular modes of production such as hunters or wage-labourers, they are defining standard instances of behaviour by utilizing the concept of a role. A cluster of roles, each defined by a set of rules, makes up a mode of production. In short, whether or not these rules are law, it is evident that a full understanding of the material base leads to a recognition of the inevitable place of rules in governing the relations of production.

This point can be perceived more graphically if we look at a typical judgment of a common law court regarding an issue connected to the relations of production. In a Scottish case, *Duke of Buccleuch* v. *Alexander Cowan and Sons* 5 S.C.214 (1866), L.R. 2 A.C. 344 (1876), the defendant paper manufacturers were polluting a stream which the aristocratic landowner who brought the action used for watering his sheep and cattle. There was a risk that the effluent in the stream would reach such a level that the water would become undrinkable by either man or beast. In former centuries the baron might have been tempted to exercise his military power to close down the factory, but by the middle of the nineteenth century even though the Border Country was fairly remote, he felt constrained to rely upon the power of the state to protect his interests. He brought an action for nuisance, that is a civil wrong or tort, seeking an order from a court which would prohibit the manufacturer from polluting the stream.

Now the law of nuisance is vague, and necessarily so. The general principle is that neighbouring landowners should behave reasonably with regard to each other, but what the law requires must depend on the circumstances. Playing a piano may be unreasonable according to the time and place of the performance. Keeping pigs in the yard may be unreasonable depending on the neighbourhood – fine in the middle of the prairies but unlawful in Manhattan. Similarly, it could not be asserted with confidence that every pollution of a stream constitutes an actionable nuisance, for what might appear monstrous in the hilly pastures of the Border Country would be considered trivial in the context of all the sewerage and industrial effluent contained in a river flowing through a city. Accordingly the opposing counsel presented different interpretations of what was reasonable in the particular context, both of them finding precedent decisions to buttress their submissions.

From a Marxist perspective, the substance of the conflict between the Duke and Alexander Cowan & Sons turned upon inconsistent uses of the productive force represented by the stream. The Duke organized an agricultural mode of production on his lands, so it was in his interest to define the primary function of streams as the provision of drinking water. On this view, any pollution of the stream would be unreasonable and therefore tortious. The paper manufacturer, on the other hand, put the stream to a different use within the industrial mode of production which he had introduced. It was in his interests to define the primary function of a stream as one of ridding the countryside of effluent and sewerage resulting from human activities. His counsel therefore submitted that there could only be a nuisance if someone was obstructing or diverting the stream from its original course.

As between these two views of the productive force, the court decided the case in favour of the Duke. It was held that some pollution was permissible, for, to be candid, even the cattle sometimes inadvertently muddied the waters. The amount of legally permissible pollution, however, should never be so great as to make the water useless for watering cattle. After considerable procedural wrangles and numerous appeals to superior courts lasting over forty years, a judicial order was issued forbidding the manufacturer to continue polluting the stream.

When we look closely at this legal rule concerning the pollution of streams, can we say that it is merely superstructural? It is a rule which directly regulates the relations of production. More precisely, it protects an agricultural mode of production from invasions of its vital productive forces by industrial enterprises. At the same time it necessarily inhibits the development of industries which use streams as a cheap cleansing process or for the disposal of effluent. Indeed, it comes as no surprise to discover that the rule against pollution was largely reversed by the end of the nineteenth century. Almost imperceptibly, as a result of a series of judgments on the point after aggressive litigation, the definition of reasonable behaviour was gradually relaxed until the law of nuisance ceased to have a substantial environmental impact on the purity of streams.[4] But until that transition had occurred the law endorsed an agricultural mode of production and resisted the introduction of industry into the countryside. The law of nuisance provided landowners with a kind of property right to use and enjoy the uncontaminated flowing waters of a stream running across their land. The agricultural mode of production both presupposed and depended upon the enforcement of that right against challengers like the Cowans. The legal rule provides the stability and reliability which any set of relations of production requires in order to flourish. It defines the reciprocal expectations and the basis upon which the landowner conducts his farming. In this sense relations of production have to be constituted by normative frameworks which are generally respected.

Here, then, are three reasons why Marxists should abandon the base and superstructure model. All of them are directed towards the claim that it is possible to exclude superstructural phenomena from a concept of the material base. Plamenatz contends first that it is impossible to define the relations of production without using legal terminology, and second that the property rights involved in some relations of production depend upon legal systems for their existence. Finally, I have added to these points by arguing more broadly that the material base must include a normative dimension in order for it to possess the necessary stability and reliability to last long enough for an entire social formation to arise upon it. The law, therefore, appears to function in both base and superstructure and cannot be pigeon-holed at the periphery of a social formation.

(2) Cohen's Defence

One important response to these criticisms of the base and super-structure metaphor has been put forward by G. Cohen.[5] He begins with an alteration of the terms in which the theory of historical materialism is expressed in order to counter Plamenatz's first point. Instead of defining the relations of production by reference to legal rights and obligations, Cohen argues that the idea can be more accurately expressed in words which avoid legal and normative connotations. He uses the concept of power to replace rights and obligations. The existence of a power is solely a question of observable fact. It denotes the ability of a person to control some aspect of the behaviour of himself or another. Thus the Duke of Buccleuch had the power to walk on his lands, and the Cowans had the power to pollute the stream. On the other hand, a right is allocated to someone not because of his physical ability to enforce it, but because authoritative rules lead us to the conclusion that the person should receive a particular benefit or suffer a detriment. The Duke of Buccleuch had the right to enjoy an unpolluted stream, even though he was unable to enforce it satisfactorily for a long time. Cohen uses the term power instead of rights in order to describe a set of production relations. For example, the Duke of Buccleuch had the power to permit his cattle to drink from the stream and graze on the hills. Similarly, an employer has the power to decide what commodities should be produced and to fix the standards of workmanship. Also the wage-labourer has the power to choose whether or not to work for a particular employer. In this fashion Cohen escapes the need to express relations within productive activities in legal terminology.

It may indeed by possible to translate all expressions of the material base from the terminology of rights to that of powers. This is likely because powers to enforce rights are usually given to the holders of rights. Obviously it would be unsatisfactory if a court were to tell the Duke of Buccleuch that he had the right to enjoy unpolluted stream water but then to decline to give him an effective remedy against the Cowans. This association between rights and powers only highlights Plamenatz's second criticism of the base and superstructure metaphor. It is evident that many of the powers which are exercised in the relations of production are dependent for their existence upon legal mechanisms of enforcement. Private ownership of property gives one the power to exclude others from enjoying the land only because the legal system provides sanctions which can be used against trespassers. Cohen admits that in a stable social formation men have the powers which compose the relations of production because the law enforces rules containing the right to exercise those powers. But he claims that in a period of transformation it is possible to distinguish what the relations of production 'really are' from what ordinarily maintains them. He explains that although an economic base appears with hindsight to be constituted by law, in fact, during its inception, it was developed through extra-legal relations. So, for example, when powerful landowners enclosed real property with the effect of dispossessing peasants of their source of livelihood, they were probably acting unlawfully. However, the ensuing reorganized form of agricultural production was quickly vindicated by the law. The courts and legislature soon recognized absolute rights of property ownership rather than maintaining the ancient customary rights and privileges shared by the villagers in common. At the same time the peasants were forced to become wage-labourers in the countryside and the towns, and eventually this form of economic arrangement was condoned by the development of rules to govern the contract to employment. The sequence of events which forms a regular pattern is, on this view, an extra-legal exercise of power followed by consolidation of the new position in the law. Thus the material base can be understood independently of legal concepts and is seen to be a determining influence upon the law. A similar process might be said to have occurred in relation to the industrial use of streams. Manufacturers used the streams unlawfully at the beginning, but because of the speed of their expansion and the long delays of litigation, by the time the law of nuisance was applied to them in cases such as the *Duke of Buccleuch* v. *Alexander Cowan & Sons* it was really too late. Many had begun to consider the pollution of rivers and streams as a reasonable usage.

By this ingenious combination of terminological change and an emphasis upon periods of social transformation, Cohen creates a powerful defence of the traditional concepts of historical materialism. Plamenatz's first criticism of the base and super-structure metaphor is met by a variation in the mode of expression. His second point is admitted in so far as it refers to mature social formations where indeed the law guarantees the powers exercised in a mode of production. A distinction between legal rights and powers emerges, however, when we discover unlawful exercise of force at the inception of new production arrangements. Here the base is divorced from legal rights, which are only created subsequently in order to stabilize and protect the new relations of production. Cohen, therefore, successfully meets Plamenatz's criticism that it is impossible to disentangle the legal superstructure from the material base.

Yet there remains my third criticism of concepts of the material base which exclude a normative element. To reduce the relations of production to a transient power relation ignores the need for rules to define reciprocal expectations within economic arrangements. Especially in the context of exchanges, the degree of trust required for a pattern of commerce to emerge presupposes a framework of accepted rules of fair conduct. It is insufficient that the Duke of Buccleuch should have the power to water his cattle: he also needs respect for his claim to be a generally accepted norm in the community, for frequent violations of the law of nuisance could undermine the system of production.

Cohen could try to defend his theory against this third criticism by continuing to distinguish between powers on the one hand and norms which arise subsequently on the other. Yet, at this point in the debate it is important to stand back and look at the direction of the argument. Cohen insists that the relations of production are a momentary power relation which quickly comes under the governance of superstructural rules. For him this is a satisfactory definition of the material base because it fits into his general explanation of the base and superstructure metaphor. It will be recalled that Cohen adopts a kind of crude materialism which he describes as functionalism. By this term he means that the superstructure has the content it does because that content is required to suit the relations of production. Thus the normative superstructure arises in order to suit the temporary power nexus. My earlier objection to this and other similar interpretations of historical materialism was that they fail to explain how the material base generates the conscious ideas which are behind the creation of superstructural institutions. Without an account of the material determination of conscious action and ideologies, there is nothing to tie the development of the superstructure to the evolution of the material base. Men would be free to impose laws which completely obstruct the passage towards Communism. Crude materialist theories merely assert that conscious action is determined without locating the mechanisms by which this is effected. Cohen simply claims that superstructural norms arise to accommodate the exercise of power but gives no reason to suggest why this happens.

In order to fill this gap in the theory of historical materialism, I suggested that the main themes of the dominant ideology must be determined by the practices in the relations of production. This solution was in accordance with Marx's own theory of ideology and supported a sophisticated version of the traditional class instrumentalist theory of law. Such an explanation of the ideological determination of the superstructure leads us to prefer a more complex view of the relations of production than the interpretation proffered by Cohen. A dominant ideology with the potential to shape a social formation could only arise from settled social practices where norms of behaviour had established a degree of regularity of behaviour within which persistent conceptions of the world could emerge. This ideology could not arise from the kind of transitory power relations by which Cohen characterizes the material base. Thus if my objections to crude materialist interpretations of the base and superstructure metaphor were sound, then we are also forced to reject Cohen's argument that norms can be excluded from a conception of the material base.

(3) Rules in the Relations of Production.

Once it is conceded that rules constitute a part of the material base, we return to the initial problem of disentangling superstructural elements from the relations of production. A new dominant ideology can only arise and govern changes in the law if the social practices in the relations of production have altered. Yet for those practices to have changed there must have been a variation in the norms governing them. If those norms are legal, then we find ourselves trapped in a vicious circle: the law can only change on this theory if it has already been altered. For example, a law of contract which is necessary for the widespread exchange of commodities can only arise if there is a favourable dominant ideology. But that ideology can only occur where there is a general pattern of commodity exchange. The paradoxical consequence of this interpretation of the base and superstructure model is that for a law of contract to emerge it must already exist!

In strict logic it is possible to escape this trap if we distinguish between law and other kinds of norms.[6] A variety of norms are present in every society, including customs, morals, etiquette, and law. The base and superstructure metaphor can be preserved if it is argued that only informal customary rules constitute the relations of production and that legal rules are excluded. In the case of the Duke of Buccleuch, for example, the informal social rule against pollution of streams existed long before it was seriously threatened by industry. Such social rules composed the property relations of the material base. Legal rules arise only when the social rules become controversial and deviant behaviour is energetically defended. In order to resolve the dispute an authoritative body such as a court will decide what standard of behaviour is appropriate. The court will endorse the existing social rules because they are part of the dominant ideology which has arisen upon the relations of production. The social rules both constitute the relations of production and amount to an interpretation and expression of them.

This defence of the base and superstructure metaphor is close to that suggested by Cohen but with the vital difference that norms compose the relations of production. At first sight this reformulation appears promising. It meets the objections to non-normative conceptions of the relations of production whilst avoiding the introduction of legal rules into the material base. Despite its theoretical neatness, two important objections persist.

In the first place, this solution relies upon the existence of a clear distinction between social and legal rules. Such a demarcation is often extremely difficult to draw. The status of customary rules in tribal societies is, for example, ambiguous. They often lack features commonly associated with law such as institutionalized mechanisms for adjudication and arrangements for effecting deliberate changes in the rules. On the other hand, tribal customs tend to share some characteristics with law such as sanctions in the event of deviance. In modern society also there will often be uncertainty where law begins and custom leaves off. In *Sagar* v. *Ridelhalgh & Sons* we looked at the provisions of a contract which included a customary practice of making deductions from pay. Are the terms of the contract legal rules or customs and standards which conform to law? Similarly, the rules laid down by management in a factory are analogous to law, and given the likelihood of their endorsement by a court if they are challenged, from the perspective of an employee the factory rules are as good as law. In the light of these overlapping character-istics of form and function, to say that some customary rules are not law inevitably involves a selective definition of law, and the principal motivation behind this choice could only be to preserve the integrity of the thesis that law is always superstructural.

A second difficulty for the proposed explanation of the base and superstructure model is created by the role played by legal rules in the relations of production. It has been frequently acknowledged above that the rules which constitute the relations of production in modern society are legal in form. The basic unit of capitalism, exchange of commodities, is expressed, constituted, and given the necessary stability and reliability by the law of contract. Similarly, landowners rely upon the law of tort to protect their exclusive right to exploit their property. If legal rules are in fact the norms which compose the material base, then despite the theoretical neatness of the claim that the relations of production are composed of non-legal rules, it can be falsified empirically.

In the face of these two powerful objections, Marxism is inevitably forced to search for a more complex metaphor for the materialist thesis. The elementary functional and spatial distinctions between base and superstructure break down under close scrutiny. The legal form of social institution pops up in the relations of production at the same time as it regulates the state apparatus. No plausible distinctions can be drawn between the rules regulating the economy and the state with regard to either their appearance and formal qualities or their functions. Despite this set-back for the traditional formulation of the theory of historical materialism, I think the gist of the Marxist analysis of social formations can be preserved.

My strategy is to weaken the topological metaphors and to concentrate upon the historical development of social formations. It is possible to accept that legal rules both express and constitute the relations of production, but to argue also that these laws are determined by the relations of production. How can this paradoxical interpretation of historical materialism be justified? The answer begins once again in the Marxist theory of ideology.

It should be remembered that Marxists hold that values, beliefs and motivations for conscious action are produced through the experience of practical activity. It was argued in the previous chapter that if law is a form of conscious social regulation then it will be inspired by the dominant ideologies which emerge from social practices occurring in the mode of production. These ideologies will be articulated initially in customary rules and moral standards. Legal regulation inevitably coincides with such norms of behaviour as it is merely a more precise and positive articulation of the requirements of the dominant ideology.

The special quality of law, however, is that, once a formal legal rule has been announced, it often appears to subsume the existing customs within itself, for members of the society look henceforth to the legal rule rather than the customary practices for guidance. For example, in the community of hunter-gatherers the custom of hunting together in groups would naturally become a cornerstone of the relations of production. If ever a conflict arose about this customary rule, the community, if it was destined to survive, would have to develop mechanisms to control deviance such as mediation, appeals to magic, or fighting. One sophisticated method of settling disputes is to create institutions which make authoritative declarations on the content of the community's rules of behaviour. Whatever technique is used, the result will be the endorsement of a particular standard found in the dominant ideology; thus in the case of the hunting community, the rule would require general participation in the capture of prey. Once the rule has been announced, however, anyone who questions the co-operative hunting practices in the relations of production will be referred not to the customary nature of the behaviour but rather to any authoritative determination which governs those activities. Similarly, the answer to Mr Sagar's question "what right have my employers got to make deductions from pay for poor workmanship?", is no longer "because we have always done so", but now after the legal determination of the dispute the response is "the practice is justified by a rule of behaviour legitimately promulgated by an authoritative agency of the community which has the power to enforce its decision". In this sense, the legal rule (in so far as it is publicly announced and positively articulated) will subsume existing customs leaving them redundant as guides to correct behaviour. The law is a metanormative phenomenon because it overlays and swallows up existing standards of conduct.

But why does this metanormative dimension of law help us to explain how law can both be a superstructural phenomenon and also constitute the relations of production? The answer is simple. The origin of legal rules is found, according to Marxism, in the dominant ideology as it is represented in customary standards of behaviour. The content of the law is determined by this dominant ideology and therefore legal rules are superstructural in form. Nevertheless the metanormative quality of law then places the legal rules in the position of closely regulating the relations of production, to the extent of being the sole institution giving them concrete form and detailed articulation. Thus law is superstructural in origin but because of its metanormative quality it then may function in the material base.

Furthermore, the legal rules serve as a material basis from which additional ideologies may arise, and in a snowball effect the whole social formation will slowly emerge. For example, during bartering and exchanges of commodities, customary conceptions about the appropriate standards to observe will develop. This ideology will then provide the substance for legal regulation of disputes and the organization of the mode of production. In turn, the more exact definitions of obligations within a set of relations of production provided by the law will create the opportunity for the development of further superstructural phenomena, such as complex legal doctrines to govern sophisticated contracts.

Thus the connection between base and superstructure is one of ideological derivation and incremental growth. The superstructure is derived from the relations of production because it is created according to the dictates of the dominant ideology which is produced in practices associated with the relations of production. Laws which are superstructural in origin then serve as rules to govern the material base, and because they render the customs irrelevant to social behaviour, the legal rules actually constitute, define, and express the relations of production. This close regulation then permits, perhaps encourages, further complicated social structures to arise. The pattern of interaction between base and superstructure is cumulative rather than circular. The process of accumulating a sophisticated political and cultural life will continue with the aid of law until a revolution transforms the relations of production abruptly, and then a new dominant ideology will arise to determine gradually the content of another social formation.

An incidental advantage of this formulation of the base and superstructure model is that it becomes unnecessary to distinguish clearly between social rules and legal rules once it is conceded that the base and superstructure do not always differ in form or function. Legal rules may be superstructural in origin and then serve as part of the material base, and no importance need be attached to the term law. Thus whether or not the rules governing the capture of prey in the hunter-gatherer society are custom or law is a matter of indifference. The rules will be superstructural in origin even though they now constitute and govern the productive activities.

The consequence of this interpretation of historical materialism is that it makes little sense to ask if some of the laws we have looked at are in the base or the superstructure. There is no point in puzzling over the rules of private nuisance in the case of the Duke of Buccleuch to decide whether the standards of reasonable behaviour constitute or reflect the relations of production. Instead, the laws should be regarded as the product of cumulative interaction between productive activities and conscious regulations. Initially the legal standards were derived from an ideology which emerged from informal social practices involved in grazing livestock. The laws then subsumed the customs of the district and both articulated them in more detail and authoritatively endorsed them as correct. Thus the rule against pollution was certainly superstructural in origin, but rapidly it began to function as a rule constituting the relations of production. Of course, this analysis destroys the simplicity of traditional interpretations of the base and superstructure metaphor, but it has the merits of preserving the key element of material determination and providing a persuasive interpretation of the origins and content of laws.

(4) A concept of Law

It is time to reflect for a moment upon the concept of law which has emerged from this Marxist analysis of society. Although I have not been concerned to provide a definition of law, or even to select a paradigm instance of legal phenomena, a picture of the main functions of legal systems and law-like institutions has been slowly emerging in the preceding chapters, and once the standard functions of an institution have been identified, an inevitable consequence is that a concept of law is implied. This concept is one which delineates the least complex form of social institution which can fulfil the standard functions of law satisfactorily. It is not a conception of law which encompasses all the dimensions of recognized legal systems. Nor is it one which clearly distinguishes law from all other kinds of social rules and institutions which may serve identical purposes. It is rather the simplest example of the phenomenon, an archetype from which sophisticated systems are derived.

Our starting-point for a description of the functions of law was the traditional Marxist claim that law is an instrument of class oppression. This traditional analysis of law led to the adoption by Marxists of an imperativist image of law. For writers like Lenin, the legal system was a coercive organization which issued orders backed by threats in the form of criminal codes. Together with the remainder of the State apparatus the law ensured that the wishes of the dominant class were carried out. Legal rules were in the basic form of commands addressed to the masses to do or to abstain from doing something, and the significance of law in a society depended entirely upon its potential to affect behaviour by threats of sanctions. Yet this traditional imperativist concept of law must now be rejected in the light of the broader functions of law which have been identified in the preceding chapters.

From our investigation of social formations according to the principles of historical materialism two overlapping functions of law have been emphasized. In the first place law resolves conflicts within a community by approving and enforcing standards of behaviour which are consistent with the dominant ideology. A second function of law is ideological. Legal institutions are some of the most important purveyors of the dominant ideology. Not only do the judges operate as articulate mouthpieces for the dominant ideology, but also the whole of legal discourse expresses concepts such as private ownership which become inculcated in the values of every citizen through their constant exposure to legal rhetoric.

This change in the Marxist explanation of the functions of law is related to transitions in the Marxist analysis of how social order is established. The traditional Marxist perspective found in the Communist Manifesto emphasized the tensions created by class struggle. Social order was seen as a problem of political stability. The role of law was to provide a system of control of deviant behaviour. Law and state were indissoluble, both functioning to suppress the subordinate classes. The corresponding imperativist concept of law first received a modification when it was recognized that political stability is achieved as much through ideological hegemony as through coercion. Gramsci introduced the Marxist tradition to the notion that the dominant class secure consent to the social system by using various institutions such as schools, the media, and the courts to propagate ideologies which legitimate their hold on power. Once this ideological function of law is accepted then the simple imperativist concept becomes unsatisfactory. In addition, a normative dimension must be introduced. Law not only coerces men into good behaviour, but it articulates and advertises a particular definition of the right which is in tune with the dominant ideology. Law has a normative element in that it provides authoritative standards which citizens use to criticize others and to guide their own behaviour.[7]

Yet this concept of law still rests on a myopic view of the problem of social order. There is a more fundamental question than how law helps to secure control over a system of domination. We may ask how the mode of production and its corresponding division between social classes is originally constructed, and what permits men to combine together in associations and to establish relations of production which work? Many features of social life are prerequisites here, most notably the ability to communicate through signs and language, but in this chapter we have focused on the part played by customary rules and law in the process of establishing a set of relations of production. We found that norms of both kinds defined social roles in the productive activities and discouraged deviant behaviour which might upset the arrangements. The specific functions of law and legal institutions which we identified were to settle conflicts about appropriate standards of behaviour and to provide the stability and reliability necessary for the mode of production to become firmly established. What is the corresponding conception of law which emerges from this analysis of its main functions?

A minimal conception of law must include a body whose pronouncements about the proper standards of behaviour are regarded as authoritative. Furthermore, this body must be in a position to secure compliance to those rules of conduct by the exercise of force and persuasion. At the same time this body must articulate norms which are in tune with the dominant ideology, and the best way of ensuring this connection is to endorse existing customs and social rules. Such a body would then be in a position to satisfy the two principal functions of law indicated by Marxism.

Examples of such simple legal institutions are rare in modern legal systems. One consequence of the separation of powers between lawmakers and judges is that the courts have to follow codes and statutes, and are prevented from deciding cases according to customary principles. These sophisticated forms of law improve upon the efficiency of simple courts by providing forward-looking, detailed, and practical regulations like the Combination Act 1800 to meet problems in advance, and more consciously organize a society around a mode of production. At the same time the rejection of customary principles as the source of law permits more open ideological conflict in the creation of legislation. Perhaps the institutions which in modern society remain closest to the minimal conception of law are Common Law courts.[8] The operation of the court in the Duke of Buccleuch's case conformed to the model in many ways. Customary standards of behaviour were used to settle a controversy about the relations of production and to ensure stability of the agricultural mode of production. The system of precedent forces the Common Law courts to distance themselves slightly from custom, but those precedents themselves were, of course, based upon practices and ideologies of earlier times.

To some it may appear strange that the basic Marxist conception of law is not in the form of a code or a regulation. These are admittedly the most common forms of law in modern society, and indubitably they influenced the early Marxists in their view of the functions of law and their corresponding imperativist image of law. But a deeper understanding of the functions of law in the relations of production and the maintenance of political order through ideological hegemony suggests that the elementary instance of law, its most basic form, is a court applying customary norms of behaviour.

5. The Prognosis for Law

In the opening chapter I identified two characteristics of Marxism. The first was a distinctive methodology in social theory. This approach has been illustrated and examined in its application to law. The second feature of Marxism was the prediction that the evolution of human civilization would culminate in Communism. It is to this forward-looking dimension that I shall now turn my attention.

Here we encounter the most notorious and controversial aspect of the Marxist theory of law: the persistent hostility which Marxists have shown towards law. This has always provided the focus of attention in writings about the Marxist theory of law. Indeed, if one were only to read standard textbooks on legal philosophy, the overwhelming impression which would be received is that all the remarks on legal phenomena uttered by Marxists have been to the effect that we would be better off without law.[1] Of course, that is an enormous distortion of Marxism. Most of this book has been devoted to a Marxist analysis of legal systems without mentioning such a theme. Nevertheless, it is true that Marxists have constantly questioned the need for law.

In fact, two closely related claims have been made by Marxists. In the first place it has been predicted that there will be no law in a Communist society. This forecast is based upon an understanding of the nature of the mode of production in a Communist society. Those relations of production and their corresponding social formation are said to be capable of existence without the support of a legal superstructure. At the end of the Capitalist era the law will simply wither away. The second argument against the necessity for law goes further: not only will law disappear under Communism, but it is also contended that legal systems represent the deepest evils of modern social formations, and that the absence of law will be a key feature of a truly free society.

Before explaining and defending those bold claims, I shall consider a preliminary attack mounted by Marxists against the contrary view that law is necessary for human civilization. This orthodoxy of modern political theory is dubbed by Marxists with the title 'fetishism of law'. This signifies that it is a mistaken assumption which leads to a distorted understanding of the world. After we have considered how this erroneous view has become so widespread and why it is false, we shall turn to the arguments which demonstrate the thesis that law is unnecessary, and that it will disappear in a Communist society.

(1) Fetishism of Law

A largely unquestioned assumption of liberal political theories is that laws make social order possible. Even when time is spent on the matter, it is quickly concluded that laws of some kind, be they customary norms or repressive codes are essential for any kind of civilization. A belief that humanity would be better off if it were rid of law is distrusted as either a monstrous falsehood propagated by anarchists or a wild Utopian dream which would turn out to be a nightmare in practice. Marxists have retorted that the assumption that human civilization and law are indissoluble is based upon a 'fetishism of law'.

What does 'fetishism of law' signify? To begin with, let us look at the term fetishism. In the ordinary use of the word a fetish is something which is believed to possess supernatural powers.[2] In the Marxist tradition, however, the word has assumed a technical sense because Marx used it to express a special idea; primarily fetishism signifies that the general ideological perception of things and social relations is to a certain extent misleading. In particular, Marx used the word to refer to occasions when there is a common tendency to reduce variegated aspects of social life into a single conceptual framework. Where diverse aspects of human relations are treated in identical terms, then such a condensation and unification will distort reality by presenting a uniform appearance. Marx invented this terminology in the course of his investigation of the basic elements of the capitalist mode of production.

In the final section of the first chapter of Capital Marx reaches the culmination of his argument about the source of value of goods or commodoties. A common view is that objects have an intrinsic worth which is reflected in the fact that sales take place for a price. Since all that is visible and tangible in an exchange transaction are the goods and the price, it is natural to assume that the source of value lies in the goods themselves. Marx argued, however, that value is only specified at that stage of the transaction, and that the origins of value lie in the labour-power which has contributed to the manufacture of the item. Thus the value of a commodity depends upon the amount of labour expended in its creation. To believe that goods have an intrinsic worth is to mistake mere appearance for reality. Admittedly labour-power is not apparently a source of value because it is not obviously present at the time of the sale. But the reality is that the price of the transaction depends upon labour-power expended in the production of the commodity. Any contrary belief is the result of a fetishism of the commodity, allowing the superficial appearance of intrinsic worth to hide reality.

Marx used the term 'commodity fetishism' in another sense as well. In this instance he highlighted an ideology which reduced many dimensions of human activity to the simple form of the production and sale of commodities. Under the capitalist mode of production, men manufacture goods not because they or their employers wish to use them to satisfy their own needs, but because the owners of the means of production intend to sell them. It seems as if everything only exists to be bought and sold, as in the game of Monopoly, where houses are only constructed to be sold and exploited, not inhabited.

This perspective upon work and productive activity is taken to the ridiculous length of treating even labour-power itself as a commodity. A man's time available for work is bought and sold in the market like any other object. The purchaser, a capitalist, can use labour-power like other commodities in almost any way that he happens to select. This is the nadir of the ideology of commodity fetishism, when a man's labour is treated like a thing. This is the culmination of the process of reducing human relations to commodity exchanges.

It is clear from this brief exposition of Marx's theory of commodity fetishism that he used the term in several senses. As well as the persistent theme that fetishism involves a distortion of reality, there is the vital aspect of the assimilation of many diverse features of social life within a unified ideological category. Commodity fetishism is, of course, an accurate ideology to the extent that in practice labour-power is handled as a commodity under the capitalist mode of production, but Marx protested that it was an insidious and misleading way of thinking about and treating other men. Now the question arises of how this concept of fetishism is connected to law?

Marx and Engels did not expressly make any direct link, but they often presented ideas about law containing similar themes.[3] Some Marxists, however, have explicitly used the term fetishism to refer to attitudes towards the legal form. Wherever law is raised to the position of being the foundation-stone of a social formation, or being the cause of a social transformation, Marxists perceive the fetishism of law at work. We saw in the previous chapter that the base and superstructure metaphor provides the key theme in historical materialism. We established that traditional Marxist analyses of social formations located law as a superstructural phenomenon determined in its form and content by the material base. Thus, economic and social relations preceded legal regulation and were not constituted by laws. So to explain the origins of capitalism, for example, Marxists looked for transitions in the relations of production, and attacked arguments which were designed to show that the presence of a law of contract to govern commodity exchange was a vital contributory factor in the evolution of the capitalist mode of production. The fetishism of law is the converse belief that law is vital. This fetishism arises because of the manner in which law touches upon every aspect of social life. It defines, analyses, and regulates all manner of relations, and ordinary citizens learn to interpret social phenomena according to legal categories. Yet the key point in historical materialism is that the law is not basic to social structures, and that to believe that all these social relations are created by and depend upon law is to mistake the appearance of legal omnicompetence for the reality of material determinism. As Pashukanis put the argument, social relations are not commanded by law.[4] He contended that because the relation between debtor and creditor is generally only understood within a legal framework, this suggests that law is the basis of social life and commercial intercourse. According to Marxism, however, this legal relation is determined by deeper elements in the social formation.

The belief in the priority of law is dubbed legal fetishism not only because it mistakes the distorted appearance for reality, but also because of what Marxists consider the ridiculous lengths to which this ideology is taken. Balbus illustrates this point with a refrain which his students repeat to him each year: "If we didn't have the Law everyone would kill each other".[5] This phrase supposes that men are naturally minded to murder, loot, and ravage, and that law provides the only reason why they desist from savagery. Plainly the reasons for non-violent conduct are more complex. Other norms of morality and custom serve as guides to action and discourage disruptive behaviour. By portraying law as the last bastion against anarchy, the fetishism of law is developed to an absurd degree.

In this sense of legal fetishism, the point which Marxists are making is that law is raised to a degree of importance in analyses of the composition and determination of social formations which is undeserved. If the principles of historical materialism are correct then law is superstructural, reflecting other more essential features of a social formation. It will be evident that this definition of legal fetishism depends upon a traditional view of the base and superstructure metaphor. The complaint of Marxists about legal fetishism is concerned with a prevalent ideology which fails to appreciate the superstructural quality of legal institutions. Yet if the criticisms of the base and superstructure metaphor raised in the previous chapter are correct then the Marxist objection to legal fetishism must also be modified.

Once we view law as superstructural in origin, as I suggested above, but accept that law constitutes a part of the material base giving it the necessary stability and reliability, then Marxism must itself move a substantial way towards legal fetishism. Legal rules do constitute the basis of a social structure even though they are derived from more fundamental social practices originally. But Marxists need not follow legal fetishism into the wilder excesses of that ideology. Marxists can accept that other social rules as well as laws serve to constitute the foundation for a social formation and to preserve social order. The general attack on legal fetishism is, however, considerably weakened as a result of our re-formulation of the base and superstructure model. If our view of this basic tenet of historical materialism is accepted, then it is wrong for Marxists to ridicule political philosophies which assume the necessity for law, though they need not concur with them in their entirety.

There are, however, a number of other senses in which the term legal fetishism is used. One example is where legal fetishism refers to the tendency to describe all forms of social rules as law. This approach has long bedevilled legal anthropology. It is more than likely prompted by a belief in the necessity for law: once legal institutions are earmarked as essential components of a social formation, then customary rules and other standards which help to establish social order are treated as law. Marxists need not, and have not, agreed. Customary rules may satisfactorily provide the normative basis for a set of relations of production until major conflicts arise. Indeed, as we noticed in *Sagar* v. *Ridehalgh,* in societies with sophisticated legal systems, the established customs will provide the flesh around the bare bones of the legal definitions of economic relations. The belief that law is essential may be more credible because of law's displacement force, or what I have called its metanormative quality. But whatever the cause of this reductionist kind of legal fetishism, there seems to be no reason for Marxists to follow suit.

A third sense of legal fetishism is the idea that there is a unique, distinct phenomenon, which is identifiable as law. In other words, there is an essence of law which is to be discovered in certain characteristic institutional arrangements and methods of discourse. I have already had cause to explain that Marxists reject this type of legal fetishism. Although a Marxist concept of law can be inferred from their analysis of the functions of legal phenomena, it is always clearly stated that other social institutions may serve similar functions and share a common form. No emphasis is placed by Marxists upon the uniqueness of legal phenomena. A belief in the autonomy of legal reasoning also constitutes part of this sense of legal fetishism, and I took considerable pains to distance Marxism from this theory. At the end of that discussion in Chapter 3 I pointed out that the autonomy thesis was closely linked to legitimating ideologies which emphasized the role of law in the control of political power. This third sense of legal fetishism is similarly linked to such legitimating ideologies, for they require a clear conception of law in order to distinguish their explanation of political authority from other forms of the exercise of power.

One last usage of the term 'legal fetishism' is connected to the impact of the ideology of commodity fetishism upon the form and content of law. It is sometimes intimated that commodity fetishism is translated into law by reducing all social relations to the governance of general rules.[6] Bourgeois legal systems are described as sets of general, abstract rules of universal application, and this form of law is attributed to the influence of commodity fetishism. I doubt whether in fact this is a fair description of many parts of modern legal systems apart from Contracts. In other fields such as Torts, Real Property, Corporations, Taxation, the overwhelming characteristic of the regulations seems to be their attention to minute detail rather than abstract principle. Furthermore, the manner in which commodity fetishism could affect those other fields remains murky, and is subject to the criticism I made of ideological hegemony at the end of Chapter 4. On the other hand, a plausible link between a generality of contract law and commodity fetishism can be established. The pattern of the development of the law of contracts in the nineteenth century bears this out in two ways. First, the paradigm of an enforceable contract was considered to be the sale of goods or a bargain, and, second, other kinds of transactions such as employment, loans, collective agreements between management and labour, were assimilated to this model despite the diversity of social relations involved. It was only possible to create such a unified set of general rules because of the background ideology which Marx described as commodity fetishism. Yet to call this particular instance of ideological determination legal fetishism is obviously confusing. It would be better to describe this as the impact of commodity fetishism upon legal ideology.

The concept of legal fetishism is clearly a complex one because of its many different senses. A loose combination of the first three aspects of legal fetishism is typically used when attacking the standard liberal political theories which stress the need for law to establish social order. We have noticed how this criticism misfires somewhat as a result of the reinterpretation of the base and superstructure metaphor. We should further realize that this attack is essentially negative. It only attempts to undermine a general belief in the importance of law without giving us reason to suppose either that law will disappear or that it is unnecessary. We should now consider the positive arguments produced by Marxists to support those positions.

(2) The Withering Away of Law

The predominant argument designed to support Marxism's hostility towards law uses the principles of historical materialism to demonstrate that law is exclusively a feature or pre-Communist societies. Within this general pattern of argument, three variants have been developed. These approaches are associated with different interpretations of the principles of historical materialism.

Their respective merits depend accordingly, in my opinion, upon the coherence of their underlying view of Marxism.

Scientific Socialism

The most famous prediction that law will wither away is ascribed to Engels and Lenin. Between them they developed a tightly knit bundle of doctrines which have often been taken to represent orthodox Marxism. They emphasized that the path towards Communism could be discerned with scientific accuracy given Marx's method for the analysis of the causes of social transformations. Furthermore they pointed out that the relations of production of a Communist society would give rise to a novel social structure. They predicted that law would wither away because the functions performed by the legal system would be gradually rendered redundant. Let us retrace the details of this argument for it has often been misunderstood.

Marxism shares with many other social and political theories the belief that the ultimate society will be a socialist one. At the end of the historical evolution of human civilization there lies a Utopia. But Marxism distinguishes itself from other theories by its insistence that it can explain the material conditions under which the final revolutionary transformation from capitalism to socialism will occur. Marxists also believe that Communist society is inevitable though its precise timing is indeterminate. Marx thus considered his theory of socialism to be scientific in the sense that it was based upon a theory of history which demonstrated the inevitabilty of the kind of Communist society which he sought, whereas he dismissed other socialists as Utopian dreamers since they could not explain the material conditions of the revolutionary transformation.

What were the material determinants for the collapse of capitalism according to Marx? He recognized that capitalism permitted a greater development of the forces of production than any previous mode of production and that accounted for the success of the bourgeoisie in overthrowing the fetters of feudalism for all time. Capitalism itself, however, suffers from the problem that it cannot continue to exploit as fully as possible the available technologies and natural resources. The reason for this failure lies in the anarchic approach of the capitalist relations of production to the forces of production with the consequential tendency of the rate of profits to fall. Periodically there are crises of overproduction and these result in the collapse of organized modes of producing goods to satisfy needs. Marx reasoned that it would become apparent to everyone that a more rational, centralized, and communitarian organization of the relations of production could avoid these acute crises.

At the same time as this historical pattern is unfurling, society becomes increasingly polarized into two social classes. Economic recovery after each crisis of overproduction can only be brought about by accumulating capital into increasingly large units, for only larger units can reproduce themselves given the tendency of the rate of profit to fall. Thus ownership of the means of production becomes concentrated into fewer and fewer hands, whilst the general mass of the population is reduced to the class of wage-labourers who are forced by necessity to exercise mechanical skills in order to earn enough money to pay for their subsistence.

The economic and social preconditions for a revolutionary transformation are now present. All that remains is for the proletariat to perceive themselves as a social class and then overthrow the structure of domination and replace it with an organized communitarian system of production. The development of class consciousness occurs because the material conditions of the capitalist mode of production provide an opportunity for this ideology to be created and propagated. Although wage-labourers are estranged from each other in the production process in the sense that they each have a separate contract with the capitalist to perform their discrete tasks, necessarily the economic activity brings them together in factories. The opportunity is thus created for the formation of unions and political parties which will foster class-consciousness and form the spearhead of the revolutionary vanguard against the capitalist mode of production. It is uncertain when these political developments will occur, and so the timing of the revolution is indeterminate, but Marx was convinced of its inevitability because of the presence of all the necessary material conditions.

Perhaps wisely Marx refrained from venturing speculations about the details of the organization of a Communist society. He did submit, however, some general observations about the material base of the new social formation. It was always a distinctive part of his social theory to maintain that the new relations of production were formed in the womb of the old. There were two elements of the capitalist mode of production which Marx indicated would be developed in a Communist society. First, the move towards centralization of the organization of the mode of production found in monopoly capitalism would be completed by the whole community running every aspect of the economy. Second, the weakening links between ownership and control occurring in joint-stock companies, worker' co-operatives, and nationalized industries would be finally broken by the abolition of private ownership of the means of production.

Given this Communist mode of production, the structural determinist analysis of historical materialism could sketch in the main features of the organization of social life in the Utopian society. Most important for our purposes was the realization that all class divisions would be abolished. Everyone would share an identical position in the relations of production. There would no longer be a division between the owners of the means of production and the supressed classes. That conclusion entailed a further point that all the apparatus of class oppression would disappear. In particular the state and legal system, which according to Marxist theory were central to the process of maintaining order, would be rendered obsolete. They would wither away in a Communist society, just as the organs of living creatures disappear during the evolutionary process if they no longer serve a useful function.

Orthodox Marxism quickly disseminated the dogma that a Communist society would be able to dispense with law. Marxists therefore not only objected to the content of class instrumentalist laws in capitalist societies, but also they attacked the legal form itself because it was symptomatic of structures of domination. On the basis of scientific socialism, however, they could also assure the working class that the prognosis for law was poor. Since, according to Marxism, the final collapse of capitalism is inevitable though indeterminate in time, and the removal of systems of law is structurally determined by the form of the Communist relations of production, the remorseless progress of history ensures that the end of law is nigh.

This leading attack on the law by Marxists is, of course, based upon the class instrumentalist theory of law, and an underlying interpretation of the principles of historical materialism which emphasizes class conflict. If the state is an instrument of class oppression, and the legal system is a sector of the state apparatus, then it follows logically that not only is the law also an instrument of class oppression but also once the division of society into classes is terminated under Communism there will no longer be any need for the state and its legal system. These are the bare bones of the most famous aspect of Marxist theories about law which led to the creation of a dogma that law would wither away in a Communist society. It has been constantly repeated by critics of the regime in the USSR in order to discredit any pretensions of that state to being a Communist society. Further, it has frequently prompted countries such as China which claim to be based upon Marxist-Leninist principles to dispense with a legal system in order to help to establish their credentials as truly Communist societies.

At first sight, indubitably as a result of the commonplace fetishism of law, it may seem absurd to believe that any society can function without law. Surely there will always be problems to be dealt with by the criminal law such as thefts, sexual assaults, and vandalism? In addition, any industrial society will require rules governing the organization of the mode of production, and surely these regulations will constitute laws? These questions underscore common perplexities about the dogma that law will wither away. It smacks of anarchism and a naïve belief in the ability of men to act justly and to co-operate without coming into conflict occasionally. It must be seriously wondered how the classic Marxist theorists of law such as Engels and Lenin could have subscribed to such utopianism.

The origin of the phrase 'withering away' is found in a tract written by Engels nick-named Anti-Dühring.[7] In one passage in this book Engels set out to defend the scientific theory of how a revolutionary transformation would occur. He explained the process in broadly similar terms to those used above. When examining the bourgeois state he pointed out that it had two principal functions. At first the state was merely used to maintain the system of private ownership of the means of production which necessarily involves the task of class oppression. Later on, as the logic of capitalism is played out, the state takes over and nationalizes industries which are threatened by economic crisis. When the revolution comes the proletariat will learn from the bourgeois use of the state as a repository of capital accumulation. They will use the power of the state apparatus to gain control over all the means of production. In the ensuing classless society, however, there will be no need for the primary function performed by the state, that is class oppression. A new role will emerge which will be the administration of a planned economy by directing the production of wealth and the distribution of goods. Engels concludes that the bourgeois state will wither away because the primary function which it serves will become redundant.

It will be noticed that there is no specific reference to law in these passages which I have summarized. We may surmise that the aspects of law involved in the task of class oppression will disappear, but it may be the case that laws will become involved in the administration of things under a planned economy. Engels is not specific because he is more interested in refuting the view that nationalization is the same as socialism. He explains that nationalization is a method of staving off economic crises, and not a parliamentary road to socialism. We may doubt the plausibility of the claim that a state which nationalizes a large sector of the economy is doing something qualitatively different from the proletariat using the state to seize ownership of the means of production. But this argument does not bear directly on the role of law in an economy organized by a classless society. On that vital point Engels remains silent.

Lenin subsequently took up the defence of Engels's views in his book *The State and Revolution*.[8] He explained that Engels did not mean that the bourgeois state would wither away, but that it would be swept away by the proletariat during the revolution. After the revolution the proletariat would institute a dictatorship to crush reactionary forces, but as these declined so the proletariat state would wither away. To some extent Lenin elaborated on Engels's thesis by the introduction of Marx's view that there would be an intermediate phase of the dictatorship of the proletariat. The effect of this modification is to concede the possibility of the continuation of repressive laws after the revolution. Then, however, they will support the working class against any reactionary forces. But, together with the state, these vestiges of legal institutions will also become redundant once all resistance has been crushed.

Thus Lenin was the first to subscribe explicitly to the thesis that law will wither away in a Communist society. In later passages in *The State and Revolution* he introduces an important qualification.[9] He acknowledges that Communist society will be bound together by elementary rules of social life. He also concedes that there will be occasional violations of these norms by individuals. On the whole, however, these offenders will be prevented from committing the deviant acts by the intervention of ordinary citizens. So there will be no need for either a system of criminal courts or a police force.

The origin and status of these elementary rules of social life envisaged by Lenin are puzzling. Is he subscribing to a Natural Law theory that certain norms are intrinsic to the nature and functions of human societies? How do they arise and who defines them? What causes deviance if not political oppression and class exploitation? All these questions are left unanswered. But they are important for our inquiry because they have great bearing on the question of the withering away of law. If these elementary rules of social life are not law, what are they?

There seem to be two differentiating factors mentioned by Lenin. First, unlike the law, the social rules will not enforce the interests of a particular class. Second, the social rules will not require institutional systems for enforcement, a hallmark of modern legal systems, for the whole community will leap to defend them. Both of these reasons given for distinguishing these elementary rules of a Communist society from law assume that law can only be an instrument of class rule. It is apparently inconceivable that law could take another form. The whole point of the legal apparatus in Lenin's eyes was that it ensured social order for the benefit of the dominant class. Any other kind of normative system would not be law by definition. Given this insistence that laws must be instruments of class oppression, the thesis that the law will wither away in a Communist society is a tautology. Since there will be no social classes, any rules which are enforced cannot be law. The nature of the new social rules is left unexplained.

In sum the classic Marxist texts present a very tight analysis. It is clear that law defined as an instrument of class oppression will disappear with the demise of the class system. Yet, both Engels and Lenin recognize that some norms will remain. There will be both rules for the administration of a planned economy and elementary rules of social life. They cannot be law, however, because they do not support a system of class oppression. The whole thesis of the withering away of law rests upon the dubious definitional fiat that rules which serve any other purpose than class oppression cannot be law.

It will be apparent from earlier chapters of this book that I consider such a definition to be unduly narrow. I put forward a number of reasons for the rejection of the class instrumentalist thesis. Primarily the defect of this classic Marxist definition of law lay in its failure to appreciate that laws not only operate to repress subordinate classes, but they also serve to construct the relations of production on which these structures of class domination arise. The material basis of human societies is composed of social arrangements for the exploitation of the forces of production. Many of these arrangements are articulated and enforced by law. By limiting their perception of the function of law to the problem of coercion, the classic Marxist writers failed to realize the importance of law in helping to establish a set of relations of production.

The underlying reason for this failure is an unsatisfactory interpretation of the principles of historical materialism. Marxism is reduced to a conflict theory of social explanation with a crude instrumentalist account of conscious action. The complexities of the problem of social order and the determination of ideologies are overlooked with the consequence that the coherence of historical materialism is undermined.

Further criticisms of the class instrumentalist definition of law were made above which also tend to undermine the thesis of the withering away of law in a Communist society. Many laws govern disputes which appear far removed from the class struggle, as for example in the case of the enforcement of moral standards. It is hard to connect laws concerning abortion, drugs, homosexuality, and rape with the instrumental pursuit of their interests by the ruling class. At best a Marxist can explain the content of these legal rules as a part of the dominant ideology far removed from narrow instrumental concerns. If so, then there seems no reason to believe that these laws will wither away entirely after the revolution, though their content might indeed be drastically altered.

The truth is that the classic Marxist theorists devoted very little attention to law. They treated it casually as part of the apparatus of the state, and so they concluded that when the bourgeois state was thrown overboard the law would go too. The concession made by Lenin to avoid the charge of being a Utopian – that some social rules would remain in a Communist society – is highly revealing. In effect he acknowledges the continuation of laws but under another name because they will no longer be connected to a repressive state apparatus. The basic

Marxist texts, therefore, cannot fairly be relied upon for a wholesale rejection of the legal form, but only the form which it had taken in class societies according to a narrow instrumentalist version of Marxism.

Pashukanis

There have been other attempts to defend the thesis that law will wither away in a Communist society which try to avoid the pitfalls of the class instrumentalist conception of law. The realization that legal rules play a part in the construction of the relations of production pointed towards a more subtle defence of the thesis. Shortly after the Russian Revolution a jurist of the USSR named Pashukanis provided an interesting new explanation of why law will disappear.[10] We must consider his work in order to judge the success of his justification of the thesis of the withering away of law.

Instead of portraying law as an instrument of class oppression, Pashukanis broke decisively with his mentors by arguing that the most vital function of law lay in its vindication of individuals' rights. We have already examined how the capitalist mode of production is constituted by commodity exchanges. Pashukanis realized that for these relations of production to operate properly it is crucial that the owners of commodities should respect each other's property rights. Without this fundamental norm concerning the mutual recognition of certain rights, it would be impossible for an economic system of commodity exchanges to work. Pashukanis adopted a crude materialist explanation of how this material base of mutual respect for rights was effected into law. He said that the concept of a juridicial subject reflected the practice of individuals holding property rights. Bourgeois law, therefore, focused upon individuals as the subjects of the law, and its function was to vindicate and enforce individuals' rights. This theory has since become known as the commodity exchange theory of law.

Of course we have already encountered similar explanations of legal concepts in earlier chapters. We used the practice of commodity exchange to account for the source of the content of the Combination Act 1800, and the judgment of Miller's case. Yet there are a number of important differences between those earlier explanations and Pashukanis's commodity exchange theory of law.

In the first place, his analysis is limited to a crude materialist explanation of the content of law. As we have concluded before, such an interpretation of historical materialism lacks an account of the mechanisms by which social practices determine conscious action, and is thus fatally flawed.

Second, and consequent upon his crude materialism, Pashukanis indulged in all the vices of reductionism, that is, he purported to explain all legal rules as reflections of commodity exchange. Such accounts are sensitive to the criticism that many laws cannot be readily characterized as ideological manifestations of social practices found in the processes of production. Although the law of contracts might be regarded as a reflection of the system of commodity exchanges, the prescription of personal assaults cannot fit into the mould so easily. Pashukanis made valiant efforts to demonstrate that criminal laws were as much based upon the deep structure of the mutual recognition of rights as the civil law. Admittedly, respect for personal autonomy underlies the law of assaults, but to limit the nature of the criminal law to the mutual recognition of rights seems to ignore its role as vindicator of the dominant values and standards of a community. Pashukanis was right to emphasize the position of the individual rather than a group as the basic unit of modern legal systems. There is indeed a marked contrast between the individualistic criminal law of modern societies with its concern for personal responsibility and the systems of clan vengeance found in pre-feudal Europe. Yet the offender in a trial for an alleged assault is not punished when convicted merely because he has invaded a person's autonomy or damaged another's body; the sanction is imposed because he has violated the established norms in the community which must be upheld in order to deter other disruptions to the social order. These features of criminal law are more startlingly illustrated in cases of victimless crimes, such as the offences concerning the taking of soft drugs. Since no other person is involved, the law must be explained in terms beyond the mutual recognition of rights thesis. Similar criticisms can be voiced about other attempts to explain the form and content of legal rules by this reductionist interpretation of law.

A third and even more startling claim of the commodity exchange theory of law distinguishes it from our earlier explanation of the origins of ideologies which determine the content of law. Pashukanis insisted that the essential nature of law lay in its reflection of the deep structure of the mutual recognition of rights. No system of rules, and here he instanced railway timetables, could be law unless it conformed to the underlying pattern of respect for individual rights. There was, he argued, a distinction between laws on the one hand, and commands and regulations on the other. But how can we tell if certain norms are law or merely social rules? For example, are the complex rules governing income tax merely regulatory or are they law? The most that can be said is that this distinction remains obscure. One suggested elucidation is that mere technical rules are united by a single purpose whereas laws deal with controversies and conflicts of interest.[11] Again it is hard to know whether tax laws serve a single purpose of financing government of if they are controversial regulations governing the claims between government and individual citizens. Probably what Pashukanis had in mind here was the contrast drawn by Engels between class rule and the administration of things under a planned economy, but this distinction itself remained extremely vague and could hardly provide the analytic basis for a definition of law.

The stage is now set for the completion of Pashukanis's theory of the withering away of law. He reasoned that since rules are only law if they correspond to the model of the mutual recognition of rights, and rules only have that form when they are so determined by the capitalist mode of production, it follows that once capitalism disappears so too will law. In other words, when the system of commodity exchanges ceases to be the basis of the mode of production in a Communist society, then the normative structure associated with exchange which is termed law will necessarily wither away. The remaining vestiges of law in Russia after the Revolution could be conveniently explained as reflections of the persisting incidence of private commercial transactions which would gradually be subsumed within a planned centralized economy. Furthermore, it is implicit in the commodity exchange theory that laws could not have existed in societies which were not dependent upon commodity exchanges as the dominant mode of production. Thus all pre-capitalist civilizations only possessed laws to the extent that there were incipient commercial relations. Roman law was a reflection of the beginnings of commerce, and the modern European legal systems were a product of the huge expansion in trade. But according to Pashukanis other kinds of social formations lacked rules corresponding to the legal form. The norms of tribal societies or the system of tenures and fealty under feudalism were by definition excluded from his concept of law because they could not be reflections of commodity exchanges.

Even if we accept Pashukanis's crude materialism and his emphasis upon reductionism for a moment, it is evident that his account of the withering away of the law in a Communist society rests upon an unconvincing definition of law. In order to make his argument work, Pashukanis falls prey to one aspect of the error of legal fetishism. He is led to insist upon the existence of one unique phenomenon which can be identified as law . This is clearly a logical step in any argument which purports to demonstrate that law will wither away, for we must be able to recognize the distinctive attributes of legal systems in order to be certain that all vestiges of them have been finally buried. I have suggested above that Marxists should not accept that there is one form of social institution known as law. In broad terms the reason for avoiding this assumption is that it obscures the more important Marxist position that there are, in each historical epoch, a variety of kinds of institutions designed to preserve order and facilitate the smooth running of the relations of production to the benefit of the ruling class. Some of these arrangements have been termed law, but the usages of the word 'law' adopted by legal theorists are typically oriented towards their defence of the existing political order and the realization of the legitimating ideal of the Rule of Law. Similarly, Pashukanis manipulated a narrow definition of law in order to substantiate a rather different political claim, namely that the law would wither away in the USSR.

Estrangement

One last argument which criticizes law according to the principles of historical materialism rests on the concept of estrangement. Here the principal contention is that legal systems are the product of the estranged social relations found in the capitalist mode of production. Once the new Communist relations of production have been introduced then estrangement will end. At the same time the importance of laws will be considerably reduced and perhaps they may eventually atrophy.

To understand the meaning of estrangement we must reconsider the relations of production in modern society. The owners of the means of production confront each other and wage-labourers as possessors of commodities. They are prepared to enter into relations of exchange, and necessity forces the worker to sell his labour-power as if it were another commodity in return for wages to buy items for his subsistence. If we examine the workplace closely we find that its organization, following the dictates of the capitalist mode of production, entails the social consequence that the wage-labourers have few significant relations with each other. On a conveyor-belt system of production each worker performs a discrete task along the line. His most important relation is with the manager, who, as representative of the owners of the means of production, is empowered to hire and fire and to direct the processes of manufacture. The worker's relationship with the rest of the shop floor is incidental to his labour. He certainly has no formal legal relationship with the others, and factory discipline discourages co-operation and restrictive practices from developing along the production line. Estrangement is the term Marxists use to refer to this atomization of labour. Although a conveyor-belt mode of production may be an extreme example, all methods of producing commodities under the capitalist mode of production share the fundamental attribute of excluding any significant relationship between the workers.

The concept of estrangement comprises both a sociological discription of social relations and an insight into the ideology or social psychology generated under capitalism. As part of a sociological analysis, the idea of estrangement points to a basic structural arrangement within the work-place. No matter how much the production process is modified to permit group participation in decisions and how far industrial democracy is introduced, these formal changes will only overlay the structure of estrangement. They will constantly find themselves in tension with the deep structural impetus towards atomization.

The ideological aspect of estrangement is crucial for the Marxist theory of revolutions. It is evident that the worker who is estranged from his fellows is less likely to perceive himself as part of a class of wage-labourers. He probably regards them as competitors for wages and graspers after larger differentials rather than workers with a common group interest. Under such circumstances, according to the materialist theory of consciousness, the structuring of the capitalist mode of production inhibits the development of class-consciousness. Although workers are brought together into the factory, they are treated as individuals and are discouraged from perceiving themselves as a combined unit. As a result the working class fails to perceive itself as a class, which according to Marx, is a necessary pre-condition of the revolutionary transformation of capitalist society.

The idea of estrangement anticipates a later nineteenth-century sociological distinction drawn between types of social relations found within a group. Tönnies contrasted two kinds of group, a 'community' and a 'society'.[12] In the former there is mutual trust and agreement over the rules of social life, whereas in the latter men inhabit an atomistic social order in which social relations involve specified commitments rather than open-ended pledges. There is a similarity between the idea of estrangement in Marx's work and this later typology of varieties of social solidarity for estranged relations are characteristic of a 'society' rather than a 'community'.

Although Marx did not pursue his analysis into a developed set of distinctions about social solidarity, he did make a major contribution to the analysis of estrangement in modern society. He was enabled by his materialist theory of consciousness to locate the material determinants of the atomistic quality of bourgeois society in the structural properties of the capitalist mode of production. In the practices developed around commodity exchanges, an ideological interpretation of social relations was formed in which men regarded each other as individual possessors of property rights who entered the market to seek exchanges. We utilized this account of bourgeois ideology to explain the content of modern laws such as the Combination Act 1800 and the decision in Miller's case.

If, however, we now follow up this analysis of estranged social relations in modern society, we will discover grounds to support the Marxist hostility towards law. Our earlier description of law as an authoritative determination of the proper social rules to guide behaviour, entails the idea that the legal form is only required when there is a breakdown of consensus over the appropriate rules of behaviour. In a society of estranged social relations it is reasonable to infer that the possibilities of conflict during social interaction are increased, and this in turn reproduces the need for legal determinations of the troublesome issue. A comparison of two forms of society will elucidate this point.

In a closely knit tribal community the degree of social solidarity formed as a result of common experiences and education establishes a consensus over the rules governing social relations which are therefore rarely challenged. Hence the occurrence of authoritative determinations of conflicts is rare. In contrast, the atomization of modern society accompanies a low degree of ideological consensus. Institutionalized methods of providing solutions to disputes abound. Legal rules multiply to meet the increased frequency of conflict. So family affairs which are regulated by informal and unquestioned custom in a tribal society are governed by legal rules under capitalism. We than reach the stage of the fetishism of the law in which legal rules are seen as the basis of social life rather than an articulation and vindication of pre-existing social rules and values.

A second effect of the structurally determined estrangement of men in modern society is that the increased occurrence of conflict encourages the greater sophistication, rationalization, and organization of the legal system. If all the disputes are to be considered seriously then there must be a highly efficient set of institutions to deliberate on the appropriate rules of social behaviour. Thus certain aspects of modern legal systems in capitalist countries emerged as a result of a need created by the mode of economic organization for courts of law to establish and defend the ground rules of the social order. In concrete terms, as we have noted already, the expansion of commodity exchange as the basis for a mode of production required a reliable system for the enforcement of bargains. A body of public courts becomes essential for a society in which the standard economic relationship is an exchange carried out between two strangers at arm's length. There was no other mechanism by which the rules of behaviour in commerce could be vindicated once the trade routes became extended.

Finally, as well as providing a theory of the structural determinants of certain aspects of modern legal systems, the analysis of estrangement provides a partial justification for the belief that law will wither away in a Communist society. One of the characteristic qualities of Communism identified by Marxists is the abolition of instrumental labour and the full realization of the aim of socialization of the workplace. Under the new arrangements of production, men will co-operate together on projects of their own choice rather than performing discrete tasks alone at the direction of the manager. As a result the quality of estrangement will also be removed. Thus men will be permitted to see themselves as members of a group with a high degree of solidarity.

It follows from the premises about the connection between estrangement and law that, given a widespread consensus about the content of the social rules in a Communist society, very few authoritative determinations of rules will be required. This image of the nature of men's social relations in a Communist society seems to approximate to Lenin's vision of general observance of the elementary rules of social life. But the prediction suggested by the theory of estrangement does not support the view that all law will disappear under Communism for there may still be conflicts and transgressions even in a closely knit community. It is plain, however, that the degree of penetration of law and the need for legal institutions will be substantially reduced.

If we assess the outcome of all three arguments put forward in this section we find that none of them succeed in demonstrating the withering away of law thesis. At most these theories support the proposition that certain kinds of law will disappear, or that the amount of law will be reduced in a Communist society. The arguments raised by Lenin and Pashukanis are defective both for their unsatisfactory interpretation of the principles of historical materialism, and for their corresponding narrow view of the form and functions of law. The analysis of estrangement is, on the other hand, compatible with the interpretation of Marxism endorsed in this book and relies upon an acceptable view of legal phenomena, but, in fact, it only supports the claim that much of the paraphernalia and sophistication of modern legal systems will disappear in a Communist society, not that the law will wither away altogether.

(3) Human Nature

A second kind of argument used by Marxists to support the thesis that law is unnecessary for human civilization tackles the legal fetishism of liberal political theory directly. It is a rarely questioned assumption of this kind of political philosophy that law is an essential condition of social order and civilization. This viewpoint is common to classic thinkers like Hobbes and to recent explanations of the justification of state power such as that suggested by Nozick.[13] These philosophies are loosely based upon a prevalent conception of human nature which emphasizes men's tendency towards selfishness, greed, covetousness, and corruption. It is this pessimistic view of man which leads to justifications for the creation of the state and its legal system, for these institutions control conflict and establish conditions suitable for peace and prosperity. Even where a less pessimistic view of human nature is espoused, the limited degree of altruism to which man may lay claim entails the conclusion that certain controls upon behaviour will always be necessary to protect the person and property from attack. Thus Hart argues that for the purposes of ensuring the survival of individuals and their community, all societies will abide by rules of law and morality governing a narrow range of activities such as aggression and co-operation in the production of food.[14]

Marxists in general reject this view of human nature, and consequently must deny the conclusions which are drawn about the necessity for law. Indeed, it is a controversial question whether Marxism includes a particular conception of human nature. The sole theme in Marxist philosophy which could amount to a theory of human nature is found in Marx's early works. In a brief and incomplete series of notes and essays called the 'Paris Manuscripts' Marx discussed tangentially a concept of man.[15] He believed that the essence of human nature lay in man's quest for freedom for self-expression through labour. The manner in which Marx approached this issue was by way of an argument that modern society imposed social conditions which were totally incompatible with man's real nature. The effect of this conflict is that man becomes alienated from his true self for his search for self-affirmation is blocked. We must briefly consider this theory that man experiences alienation in modern society in order to discover whether Marxism does indeed have its own view of human nature which is distinct from the liberal tradition.

The concept of alienation may be comprehended at two levels. We have already noted how labour-power is treated as just another commodity in capitalist relations of production. The worker sells his labour in return for money, the universal commodity. During his productive hours the worker effects projects according to instructions issued by the management. Their power to issue orders derives from the owners of the means of production who use management as an agent. The work performed is instrumental in the sense that it is only done for the payment of wages and not out of any sense of personal fulfilment. Marx viewed the reduction of all labour to instrumental tasks as the ultimate degradation of man. The wage-labourer becomes in a manner of speaking alienated from himself, for on the one hand he wants to choose work which will satisfy his creative urge, but on the other hand he is forced by economic necessity to perform work for another. The choice of tasks to be performed is in turn dictated by the demands of the market rather than the preferences of the capitalist. Consequently, Marx thought that the whole relations of production under capitalism had resulted in a crazy inversion: the market now dominates men, instead of men controlling the productive activities.

Some Marxists have attached considerable importance to this theory of alienation because it has the potential to explain why the capitalist mode of production is unacceptable no matter how much the state redistributes wealth through taxation, pay-controls, and regulation of profits. It is claimed that although Marx was misled in his prediction of the progressive impoverishment of the working class, the exposure of his error leaves unscathed the fundamental Marxist critique of capitalism which rests not so much on the unequal distribution of wealth as upon the way it engenders alienation. No amount of tinkering with the form of capitalist society by social democrats will satisfy the Marxists, for man will always remain alienated from himself owing to the instrumental nature of his labour. Only in a Communist society which will end the instrumental quality of work will alienation be superceded.

At a deeper level, the theory of alienation expresses a concept of human nature. This fundamental assumption is evidenced by Marx's view that alienated styles of work entail the worst form of degradation. Why is instrumental labour so bad? Why does it alienate man? In his early works Marx assumes that the essence of man is based upon a search for self-affirmation, a desire to express himself through his productive activities. What is required by the essence of man is freedom to select tasks and methods of operation so that they satisfy the urge to personal fulfilment. The system of production under capitalism thus alienates man from his true self, or, as Marx put it following Feuerbach, from his 'species-being'. One of the essential features of a Communist society would be the abolition of alienation and the establishment of conditions suitable for the experience of real freedom.

The incorporation of the theory of alienation into Marxism is highly controversial. One problem encountered by Marxists who endorse this concept is that any such fixed notion of human nature appears to run contrary to the principles of historical materialism. If man's consciousness depends in the end upon the material circumstances of life, then there seems no scope for positing some eternal attributes of mankind such as selfishness, altruism or a capacity for love. Althusser and many others have urged that once Marx had discovered the principles of historical materialism he was forced to abandon his earlier conception of human nature expressed in the idea of species-being.[16] In other words, there was an epistemological break between the early works and the mature theory of historical materialism. These critics of the introduction of the theory of alienation into Marxism find support for their interpretation from the fact that Marx did not discuss this deep sense of alienation in Capital and his later works. The closest approach made there to proposing a conception of man is found in the discussion of estrangement.

Now the concepts of estrangement and alienation are often spoken of as one and the same idea, but in fact they are clearly distinguishable from each other. Estrangement is a sociological and psychological description of the relations experienced between workers on the shop floor. Marx referred to the concept a great deal in his mature work as an important dimension of his description of the relations of production under capitalism. He used this view of the practices and ideology of atomistic labour processes as a description of the nature of the relations established within the working class generally in order to account for the absence of class-consciousness. The theory of alienation, on the other hand, is based upon a deeper philosophical understanding of human nature. According to Marx the system of production stunts man's basic urge towards self-affirmation and expression through labour. Alienation and estrangement constitute different levels of analysis of the properties of capitalist society. What they have in common is a materialist explanation of the condition based upon the principal exchange relation under capitalism, the contract of employment. It is plain that for those Marxists who claim that the mature Marx rejected all forms of belief in a supra-historical human nature, the concept of estrangement performs a valuable service. It provides an analysis of the material process of production on which a general interpretation of capitalist society including its ideologies can be based, but it does not become embroiled in metaphysical assumptions about the essence of man.

In my view, the best answer to the question of whether or not there was an epistemological break in Marx's thinking is that Marx did not fully appreciate his predicament. In consequence, no text can be considered decisive on this matter. What can be demonstrated, however, is that there is no necessary contradiction between Marx's early concept of human nature and the later principles of historical materialism. The way in which this can be achieved is by contrasting two kinds of theories about human nature. The first, to be found in the tradition of liberal political theory, posits a set of supra-historical motivating factors on the basis of which social order is constructed. Thus Hobbes developed his conception of the Leviathan because he assumed the essential selfishness of men. A second conception of human nature found in Marxism avoids any specific genetic traits being ascribed to mankind except one. This is the minimal idea which finds the essence of man in his quest for self-affirmation through labour. How this urge for self-expression will be satisfied depends upon the material circumstances which will shape character, values, and definitions of wants. There is, however, an underlying impetus towards self-affirmation. This latter view avoids any supra-historical conception of human wants except the desire for freedom to explore one's potential. As such it is compatible with the principles of historical materialism. Indeed, as the following argument demonstrates, it may even be entailed by the theory.

In my earlier description of the elements of historical materialism, I accounted for the changes brought about in the forces of production by technological innovation by referring to the natural ingenuity of men. Inventions provide the opportunity for new relations of production to arise. Thus Marx's explanation of social evolution depends upon a view of man which asserts a natural creativity. This ability could either stem from a liberal view of human nature in which selfishness and greed motivate men towards higher technologies, or it could be explained by man's quest for self-affirmation, in which case the development of new kinds of machinery is merely one way in which this quest may be satisfied. Thus, not only is Marx's early theory of man's essential nature compatible with the mature theory of historical materialism; it may even be required to justify an underlying assumption within the theory.

Given that the theory of alienation is probably a part of the Marxist tradition, we may consider what light it throws on the critique of the legal form. Theorists who reject the necessity for law are always accused of utopianism. But the theory of alienation neatly avoids such criticism by questioning the assumptions of liberal political theory itself. The supposition that law will always be necessary rests upon beliefs about certain constant qualities of human nature such as greed and selfishness. The theory of alienation includes the assertion that the materially determined content of the human psyche may be fundamentally transformed; under the Communist relations of production a novel type of personality will emerge which will be exempt from egocentric lusts for power and wealth. Accordingly the usual reason given by liberal political philosophy for the existence of coercive systems of behavioural control like law will no longer be extant. Men will naturally agree about the proper standards of behaviour and conform to them without the need for sanctions.

Naturally the breathtaking claims of this theory of alienation have been met with considerable cynicism. It is pointed out that there are few signs in the history of the human species that the liberal assumptions about human nature are anything but truisms. Furthermore, problems of alienation certainly persist in countries which have experienced revolutions in modern times. Nevertheless the theory of alienation does enable us to attempt to meet directly the charge of utopianism which has been levelled against the Marxist theory of the withering away of law. A legal system with its structures of power over individuals can be said to represent the alienated mode of existence of modern society in its starkest form. There is apparently a fundamental conflict between the kind of freedom envisaged by Marx in his concept of the species-being and any authoritative system of selecting the rules of a community and enforcing them. Consequently, in a Communist society where true freedom will reign, law will be unnecessary and will wither away. Of course, this argument presupposes a particular concept of law, one which includes superior power relations and, perhaps, coercion rather like the concept of law put forward in the previous chapter. Fortunately it is sufficiently broad to avoid the criticism made of Lenin and Pashukanis that they deliberately utilized unreasonably narrow definitions of law to prove their argument that law would wither away in a Communist society.

Despite all these advantages, perhaps even the theory of alienation fails to provide an entirely convincing attack on the legal form. It is obviously true that a legal system entails restrictions upon individuals and therefore interferes with their freedom. But is this form of incursion necessarily antithetical to the freedom for self-affirmation which Marx had in mind in his early writings? Could it not be said that the facility for authoritative determinations of right will provide the society with a mode of settling conflicts which are bound to occur despite a widespread consensus over the elementary social rules of behaviour? Thus laws might ensure the absence of disruption of the relations of production and prevent the misuse of force, which would foster freedom for self-affirmation at least as much as it interferes with individual liberty.

This argument that legally protected liberties are a pre-condition of men enjoying true freedom to lead meaningful lives has, however, never been a Marxist view. The inspiration of Marxism has been the ambition to achieve a community which enjoys an unalienated existence without the need for state power to stifle discontent. Consequently, the legal enforcement of negative liberties will be neither possible nor necessary in a Communist society. The conflicting demands of individuality and community will be finally reconciled. In truth, the argument that negative liberties are an indispensable aspect of the pursuit of true freedom is based upon liberal presuppositions about the limited altruism of human nature and the limited possibilities of political organization which Marxists reject. The strength of this liberal criticism stems not from any incoherence within the Marxist position but from a degree of perplexity about the shape of a Communist society in which individual freedom can be realized without constraints. If we could be more confident that relations of production could be devised which avoided conflicts and abuse of advantageous positions, then a defence of the Marxist claim that law and state will wither away would be more convincing. As it is, Marxism only provides a few foggy notions about the organization of a Communist society. On the one hand, it will be a community of vast material wealth and high technology, but on the other hand men will be able to select their own tasks without legal or economic compulsion. Industry and agriculture will be organized to avoid the anarchic crises of overproduction and shortages in capitalism, yet no one will have superior power to instruct others to work at particular jobs. Material wealth will be redistributed according to need, but no state will be necessary to effect such transfers of goods. All these things may be possible, but until we have a firm idea of how the Communist relations of production will be arranged the contention that law will wither away must appear unrealistic in view of the probable opportunities for conflict and misuse of power.

Furthermore, in the light of the conclusions reached in the previous chapter, there is serious doubt whether legal rules of some kind could be excluded altogether from a Communist set of relations of production. If it is true that men require rules of behaviour in order to co-operate in productive activities and to establish peaceful communities, then to argue that legal regulation will disappear in a Communist society may be overly hasty. Obviously any repressive form of laws would be incompatible with freedom in its widest sense, but probably elementary rules of co-operation and mutual respect could not be abandoned without destroying the community entirely. The concept of freedom in Marxism does not necessarily involve the total absence of constraints, but simply the opportunity to fulfil one's potential by giving one's life a meaning though labour – and this can only take place within the productive activities of a community. Thus forms of law which symbolize our alienated mode of existence would wither away under Communism, yet it is compatible with the theory of alienation to claim that there will always remain certain fundamental norms of behaviour in any civilized community which may have to be articulated and defended by institutions analogous to courts.

Over-all, therefore, the Marxist attack upon the legal form is unconvincing. The arguments considered in the previous section tried to deduce from the premisses of historical materialism that law would disappear in a Communist society, but the most that could sensibly be claimed was that certain functions of law would be unnecessary and that there would be a reduction in the level of legal regulation of our daily lives. In this last section the theory of alienation appeared at first sight to provide us with a promising critique of the legal form, yet in the final analysis its implications are ambiguous. We have unexpectedly revealed in a novel context the paradoxical relationship between law and freedom: law both supplies the conditions for, and incidentally places limits upon, individual freedom.

6. Class Struggle and the Rule of Law

(1) The Radical's Predicament

We turn finally from theory to practice. Much of the continuing vitality of Marxism is generated by its political implications. Historical materialism provides both a theory of how capitalist society sustains itself, and, at the same time, identifies the sources of dislocation which will eventually cause its demise. Thus Marxism supplies a systematic body of critical analysis of modern society which serves as the predominant theoretical backbone for revolutionary movements throughout the world. At times factions which claim to be Marxist can demonstrate little connection between their ideas and practices and those of Marx himself. Nevertheless many of the themes of the Communist Manifesto are common to their programmes even if the principles of historical materialism may have been misunderstood or their subtleties ignored. The notoriety of Marxism rests upon this global use of its theoretical analysis of capitalism to justify programmes of radical political movements.

Marx might have been dismayed by some of the pronouncements made in his name, but he would have been delighted by the way the theory of historical materialism has excited revolutionary movements. A vital part of the materialist theory of consciousness is the contention that there is an intimate connection between theory and practice. As we saw in Chapter 3, according to Marx there is a complex reflexive effect between men's experiences and the interpretation of the world which they devise and the norms to which they adhere. It follows that only through incipient revolutionary practices such as industrial conflict can men develop understandings of modern society which may eventually bloom into full class-consciousness and revolutionary politics. Thus Marx's exposition of the theory of historical materialism was itself contingent upon social practices among the working class and the transmission and refinement of ideologies by intellectuals. In turn, the concrete formulation of Marxism in easily comprehensible forms such as the Communist Manifesto defined the practices of the working class more cogently. According to the Marxist theory of revolutions, the proletariat's ensuing self-conscious awareness of their position in a structure of class domination would then inspire them to unite as a class to transform the capitalist mode of production. Marx argued that this revolution would occur through a combination of counter-ideologies to those of the dominant class and proto-revolutionary practices. Both aspects were essential for success.

As a consequence of the materialist theory of ideology, therefore, Marxism emphasizes the importance of practices for the development of the necessary revolutionary consciousness. A premium is placed upon the vanguard of the revolutionary party selecting the best actions to be pursued. For Marxists, it is insufficient to identify the general form of the transition process and to specify the ultimate goal of a Communist society. Because of the unity of theory and practice, they insist that the revolutionary activities have to be the correct ones or else they will fail to lead to the proletariat becoming aware of their class position.

Against this background the question of the appropriate attitude which must be held towards law assumes a special significance. An erroneous interpretation of the legal form, a false perception of the function of law, a mistaken challenge or acceptance of the legal system could cost the revolutionary movement many years of delay. If a law is obeyed when it should be openly flouted in order to increase class consciousness, the progress towards a revolution will be retarded. Conversely, if it is demonstrated that obedience to the established legal order and pursuit of reforms in the law favouring the working class will bring a revolutionary situation closer, then unlawfulness will be counterproductive. It is therefore essential for Marxism to develop a precise understanding of the correct response to the legal system as part of the strategy of revolutionary politics. Of course, the importance of law should not be overestimated. Practices with regard to law can form only a segment of a revolutionary programme; to attribute greater significance to law would be to succumb to the fetishism of law. Nevertheless, because law serves important functions in modern society it must figure in any theory of revolutionary practice.

What is the correct practice to adopt with regard to law? There was surprisingly little detailed consideration of this point in the classic texts of Marxism. For the most part, in the early days it was assumed that the proper direction for the working class was to capture control of the legislature for its own purposes. This tactic was grounded in the class instrumentalist theory of law. If it was correct to analyse laws as tools of class oppression designed to preserve the capitalist mode of production from attack, then a straightforward course to pursue was to utilize this weapon against its masters. Once the possibility of social change had been demonstrated to the passive working class, Marxists hoped that the impetus generated by the struggles to achieve the reforms of the laws would explode into full-scale revolutionary politics. Thus radicals supported limited political initiatives designed to benefit the poorer sections of the community. It was, after all, the working class whom Marxists claimed to represent, so radicals could hardly object to legislation which might ameliorate their lot, no matter how much they distrusted the institutions of the bourgeois state. The result of this kind of analysis has been the periodic though hesitant Marxist support for legislative reforms, beginning with minor interventions to control the treatment of workers in the factories and ending with the Welfare State.

As time has passed, however, this reformist strategy has been increasingly viewed as a mistake. Far from hastening the revolution, the Welfare State undermines efforts to create working-class solidarity. By preventing the fullest development of the material degradation of the working class and by providing a limited immunity from the vicissitudes of economic crises, a Welfare State delays the formation of class-consciousness and thus prevents a revolutionary situation from arising. The State removes the harshest aspects of the atomization of society by caring for the sick and elderly. There is insurance against periods of unemployment caused by economic crises in the capitalist mode of production, so nearly all the population is kept above subsistence level. In addition, opportunities are afforded through a public system of education and promotion ladders for a degree of social mobility which make incentives to co-operate a meaningful promise to the working class. Many of these benefits, and hosts of others, have been won by political struggles aimed at the introduction of legislation. But from the Marxist perspective they are a mixed blessing. Immediate results are traded for long-term disabilities in forming a dynamic working-class movement. Welfare legislation obscures the structure of class domination based on the relations of production and reduces the asperity of class antagonisms. The path of reformism is thus self-defeating and Marxists are forced to doubt its claim to be the correct proto-revolutionary practice.

The class instrumentalist view of law has spawned another direction for revolutionary practice with regard to legal institutions. The reformist use of law tends to assume that the legal system is a neutral instrument. But it could be argued in a more extreme fashion that the use of the legal form necessarily always supports the ruling class in a capitalist society. Although the grounds for this belief are obscure given the real benefits to the working class effected by welfare legislation, it does push Marxists in the opposite direction to reformism. Confronted by the knowledge that a modern legal system protects a social structure containing exploitation and class domination, an alternative route to reformism is to defy law entirely. From this perspective the correct tactic is to meet institutionalized violent methods of class domination with unflinching resistance. Any consensual participation in the legal system constitutes a betrayal of one's class, for it implies an acceptance of the legitimacy of the structures of power. A violation of the law is necessarily a blow for freedom, another nail in the coffin of the crisis-ridden capitalist mode of production.

This strand of Marxist thought became prominent in radical political movements in the 1960s, particularly in universities. An intellectual ancestry was found in Lenin's insurrectionary brand of Bolshevism. It was argued that if there were systematic and general breaches of the criminal law then the bourgeois state would be forced to reveal itself as an instrument of class oppression in order to meet the challenge and an impetus would then develop for the emergence of working-class solidarity. Law, as an instrument of class oppression, was considered a suspect form of social control which would certainly disappear with the demise of capitalism. There could be no good reason for obedience to such tainted institutions. A temporary period of chaos and violence was an inevitable by-product of a revolutionary programme, so any concern for social order and self-preservation was a misplaced reactionary doctrine.

This violent political programme is no longer the centrepiece of Marxist attitudes towards legal systems that it was in the 1960s. There is a more circumspect approach towards action which breaks the law. Why has there been this turnabout? The main reason lies in the failure of insurrection as a catalyst for the development of class-consiousness. Experience has shown that the legal system has many subtle devices for undermining the solidarity of revolutionary groups. By refusing to condemn movements as a whole, and by insisting upon proof of individual guilt, the law ignores or marginalizes the claims of radical groups about collective justice and conducts the legal inquisition in a discourse which is steeped in the individualistic ideologies of bourgeois society. Furthermore, selective prosecution and victimization undermine any sense of corporateness within the working class. Revolutionary martyrs quickly become forgotten victims in a community of estranged social relations. It has been therefore found that collective violations of law lead not so much to class solidarity as to the disintegration of groups. Class conflict is thus portrayed in the legal rules and dealt with by the courts as individual gestures of defiance. As a political practice the civil disobedience of the 1960s was a failure in Marxist terms because it achieved little in the way of fostering class-consciousness.

We are now in a position to understand the radical's predicament in defining revolutionary practice with regard to law. Different strands of Marxism advocate contradictory instructions: one indicates that maximum resistance should be mounted to law as it is an instrument of class oppression, and the other urges support for legislation which benefits the working class. The dilemma faced by the radical is that there is no good reason for choosing either of these alternative strategies. Both routes fail to meet the standard of correct practice defined by Marxism which is to raise class-consciousness. If violent resistance is sustained then the criminal finds himself isolated, processed, and eventually forgotten as working-class solidarity disintegrates under the subtly destructive pressures of the legal process. Similarly, a reformist discovers that the class-consciousness generated to secure a legislative victory melts away once the battle has been won. How can a solution to this predicament be found?

(2) The Form of Law

We can best begin our inquiry by investigating the cause of the radical's predicament. The source of the problem seems to lie in the apparent neutrality of the legal system. If, on the one hand, the path of insurrection is chosen, instead of the accused becoming the unfortunate victim of repressive measures instituted by the ruling class, the owners of the means of production keep well in the background. Indeed they do not seem to be mixed up in the legal process at all. On the contrary, an autonomous body, apparently unconnected with either class, takes it upon itself to enforce the laws against a dissident. The courts and judges present themselves as agents of the community as a whole and impose the general will as it is articulated in the law. Thus a criminal trial is quite unlike a protection racket for a narrow range of interests, and accordingly the accused is denied the opportunity he seeks to denounce the partiality of the system of justice. If, on the other hand, the radical presses for legal reforms, a small gain is achieved for the working class without any widespread development of class-consciousness. Again the apparent neutrality of the legal process is highlighted for it is seen to operate to the benefit of both social classes. Hence the Marxist interpretation of the legal system as an instrument of class oppression is patently negatived.

From whence comes the apparent neutrality of the legal system? How is it that a structure of class domination can reveal itself in politics as a neutral arbiter between individuals? If Marxism is to retain its class analysis of modern society it must dissociate this appearance of impartiality from an underlying real structure of domination and exploitation. This task falls into two parts. The first is to demonstrate that the form of the state in capitalist society is to some extent independent of the control of the ruling class, but that this independence is structurally delimited so that it can never amount to an entirely neutral government over opposing forces. To maintain this thesis, which earlier we referred to as the relative autonomy of the state, it is necessary to walk a tightrope. On one side it is possible to concede too much independence to the state so that it merges into the liberal vision of a neutral arbiter between citizens. On the other side there lies the pitfall of diminishing the degree of autonomy so that an insistence upon the directness of class rule is belied by the experience of successful challenges to the exercise of economic might. A second part of the Marxist explanation of the neutral form of law is to connect the apparent impartiality of the legal system to the relatively autonomous state in capitalist societies. If we are to understand the power of the law to deradicalize the working class and to place an ideological grid over class struggle which portrays collective rebellion as individual acts of deviance, we must follow this two stage route, for it promises to reveal the Marxist explanation of the form of legal institutions in modern society.

The Marxist analysis of the relative autonomy of the state starts with a conceptualization of a fundamental division which men experience in their social activities. In one dimension of their lives they encounter relations of power and political struggles for domination. At the same time, but in a collection of practices divorced from politics, they enter into social and economic relations which have no necessary connection to the ties of political domination. Indeed, a person with superior political power may have no other kinds of social and economic relations with his inferiors. Thus, in principle, a president or prime minister does not have to gain power through ownership of a substantial percentage of the means of production. Conversely, a wealthy financier or major stockholder will not necessarily have direct access to political power. Marx, following Hegel, termed this dichotomy found in modern society the separation of the State from civil society.[1]

The similarity with Hegel ends, however, with the common analytical category. Marx refused to accept Hegel's claim that this feature of capitalist society represents the achievement of the ultimate goal in history. He realised that the characteristic separation of State from civil society in capitalist countries was materially determined by the relations of production and supported structures of domination much like other historical forms of social organization. There is nothing special about the independence of political institutions from economic power. Certainly the state cannot claim to be the universal representative or an impartial arbiter between all conflicting interests. Marx was sure that the bourgeois state was simply another form of class domination, although this variation was much more subtle than previous structures of power because it maintained the appearance of autonomy from economic interests. Thus politicians and judges were not obviously the lackies of the ruling class. Furthermore, politics provided opportunities for the proletariat to use the state to secure limited benefits. How then does Marxism set about explicating the connection between the system of power in bourgeois society and the material relations of production? Can this explanation be made in such a way that it successfully walks the tightrope alluded to above?

Marx never fulfilled his ambition of providing a mature theory of the State in capitalist society according to the principles of historical materialism. Most of his writings about the separation between economics and politics are found in his early works in note form. A considerable number of modern Marxist studies, however, have been devoted to the unravelling of the mysteries of the relative autonomy of the bourgeois state.[2] The most promising analyses begin with an examination of the properties of the material base in true fidelity to the methodology of historical materialism. We have already noted that the key relation in the capitalist mode of production is the exchange of commodities. Marx demonstrated that the source of the reproduction of capital lay in the system of exchanges. The capitalist mode of production is distinctive because of the absence in the relations of production of any need for direct compulsion to work to be imposed by the owners of the means of production on the proletariat. There is no need to tie labourers to the land as serfs were under feudalism, nor to bind a worker to another person, as his slave was under the ancient civilizations, in order to ensure that their productive labour is appropriated by the dominant class. Capitalism relies primarily on the dull compulsion of economic necessity to preserve the continuity of the process by which surplus value is extracted. In pre-capitalist systems the State was required to support the economic structures of domination through the enforcement of laws of status, for otherwise the surplus value would not be regularly transferred to the ruling class. But the capitalist mode of production has no need for such a function to be performed by the state. All that the powerful must do in order to protect the relations of production is to guarantee the inviolability of private property and to provide a reliable system for the enforcement of contracts which transfer ownership in commodities. This is the night-watchman state of liberal political theory.

The logic of the capitalist mode of production thus explains why it is possible to have a relatively autonomous state in modern society, whilst in pre-capitalist communities there was always a close connection between state power and the power derived from ownership of the means of production. It also explains the revelation of social classes in a purely economic form under the capitalist mode of production for the first time. Hitherto social classes had been mixed up with legal definitions of status, for the system of ranks endorsed by the law determined ownership of the means of production and the distribution of surplus value, thereby maintaining the position of the dominant class. Under the capitalist mode of production, however, the way is clear for a purely economic interpretation of class position unencumbered by legal differentiations. Both employer and worker are equal before the law in their power to make contracts and own property. The system of commodity exchange allows the owner of the means of production to reproduce capital without the aid of legal coercive measures including definitions of social status.

This analysis of the logic of the relations under the capitalist mode of production demonstrates the structural compatibility of a relatively autonomous state with the reproduction of capital. It was technically unnecessary to place labourers under bonds more intricately tied than a simple contract. But a further question yet remains unanswered. Why did the bourgeoisie reject the use of political repression to support their position and instead give preference to the liberal state? In part the answer is that they did not relinquish such powers easily. It was only in the middle of the nineteenth century that the recognizable equality of a contract of employment replaced the legal relations of domination contained in an apprenticeship or household service as the general legal form of the performance of labour for another, and, in fact, it was as late as 1875 in England that criminal punishments for breach of contracts of employment by workers were abolished, though of course employers were never similarly vulnerable to criminal liability.[3] But on the whole there was a progression towards a liberal state which separated economic might from political power. What accounts for this choice of form of government?

Again we may contrast feudalism with capitalism to perceive the origins of the liberal state. The system of ranks under feudalism was based upon the need for political intervention in an agricultural mode of production; the resulting orders of hierarchy provided structures of political authority as well as the preservation of economic domination. The class of entrepreneurs, however, lacked any natural mechanisms for establishing systems of authority amongst themselves for they came equally to the market-place to exchange their wares. The introduction of any despot or oligarchy would threaten this equality by giving political power to only a fraction of the dominant class. Thus an impartial arbiter within the bourgeoisie was required. Power had to be held by a representative of the entire class and yet by one who stood above them all in order to maintain order in the market-place. A solution to this problem of political power was found both in the absolute dictator or Leviathan and then, more satisfactorily, in parliamentary democracy.

Of course, the historical development from feudalism to capitalism with their corresponding political structures was not sudden, nor was it clear cut. The new mode of production was resisted and its structures of power only emerged after lengthy political struggles. There were intermediate periods such as the 'Standestaat' when the declining aristocracy shared power to some extent with the emergent bourgeoisie. All that it has been possible to refer to here is the broad structural determinant of the form of the bourgeois state. The historical details are important for a full understanding of the origins, varieties, and limitations of the modern state. Our more immediate concern is with the main features of the resulting system of power. The real basis for the relative autonomy of the state lies in the logic of the capitalist mode of production. The additional impartiality of the framework of political institutions results from the requirement of the owners of the means of production to share power equally among themselves. No single group can retain a privileged position. Power over them must be exercised impartially through independent bodies. Here is the source of the neutrality of the modern state.

But Marxists continue to insist that the state is only relatively autonomous, and only impartial between members or fractions of the ruling class. It is not an organization of power which is meant to be shared completely democratically. It is fundamentally a committee of the ruling class. The limits upon state action stem from the power wielded by owners of the means of production, but although they need state power to protect their possession of the means of production, they will not allow that power to be abused. In our earlier discussion of the relatively autonomous state we noted that the ruling class maintain their hold on the reins of power indirectly both through the use of economic coercion and by ideological manipulation. These steering mechanisms are largely beyond the purview of this book since they hardly concern law at all. The sole exception is the ideological role played by legal institutions discussed in Chapter 3. The relatively autonomous state does have, however, many characteristics which tie it indissolubly to law.

Associated with the structurally determined neutral quality of political institutions there is a particular form of law. In the first place, the separation of State from civil society leads to the use of public and positive laws. In order to communicate with citizens participating in civil society the State must issue directives in a public rather than a covert fashion. It is best also if the laws are written down in a readily accessible form so that everyone can have the opportunity to comply with them. Unwritten vague standards which are only familiar within the organs of government would clearly be ineffective. We find, therefore, that as the modern separation of the State from civil society takes place, each society alters the form of its laws from customary obscure standards to public positive rules. Thus the Code Napoleon swept away the customary laws of the 'Ancien Régime' in France; and in the Common Law world the legal rules became intelligible through the publication of case reports and a firm doctrine of precedent, or, often, the common law was superseded by statutes.

Another feature of modern legal systems which seems entirely natural in modern society is the superiority of law over all other normative systems. Yet the hegemony of the legal institutions of the State over other rule-making systems is the recent product of a political battle. In a feudal society there were competing systems of rules emanating from different organizations. There were tensions between centralized monarchical power and the centrifugal tendencies of the nobility to assert their own dominance within territorial limits. There were also clashes between religious and secular systems of norms. In contrast, the sovereignty of legislation throughout the nation state is firmly established in capitalist societies. There is no serious challenge to the legitimacy of the State's claim to be empowered to legislate on any matter. Of course there are disputes over the advisability of the introduction of laws, but the authority of the State to override all other normative systems is not doubted. The reason behind the development of legal sovereignty lies in the bourgeois fear of a reversion to autocratic power and an end to the freedom of the market-place. The rules of bourgeois society had to be given the authority to stifle all claims to privilege, including any claim to a prerogative of making binding rules to govern the behaviour of citizens. Thus the pursuit of sovereignty for the legal system was an act of social levelling committed by the bourgeoisie against the former dominant classes such as the aristocracy.

Because the system of political power is so dependent upon public and positive laws it is often referred to by the term the Rule of Law, which is at once a description of the structure of the State and an ideal. There are three strands of moral judgment contained in the ideal. First, it symbolizes a commitment to the preservation of the neutrality of the State between classes and interest groups. Power is to be given to those who satisfy constitutional requirements which are neutral between persons for they ignore economic might or claims of privilege. Second, the laws are sovereign in their determination of the issues of who should hold political power and how it can be exercised. A constitution will specify procedures by which rules to govern the people are created, and no person may arrogate to himself the power to ignore them or to dispense with laws without due process. The Rule of Law insists that the legal procedures be followed even at the cost of considerable inconvenience to the dominant class. Finally, the laws are available and capable of being readily understood, and are enforced according to their obvious meaning. Both the official and the citizen must be able to discover their respective rights and then act upon them with the confidence that, if necessary, the courts would uphold them.

Many legal philosophers have realized that the ideology of the Rule of Law encourages us to view the form of law in a particular way. An instrumentalist image of laws would not accord with this ideal, for the law is characterized as a set of rules above petty political conflict and remote from the control of particular groups or classes. Instead, two features of the form of law in modern society are emphasized. In the first place, legal procedures and practices are oriented towards an attempt to provide justice according to rules applicable to everyone rather than an assessment of the merits of each case in the light of the behaviour and needs of the parties. Thus the principal virtue of justice is to treat like cases alike, and not to venture afield into questions of social justice involving the distribution of wealth and power. Cases must be decided according to rules rather than judicial appreciations of what will serve the interests of particular groups and individuals. A second complementary feature of the form of law in modern society is a belief in the autonomy of legal thought. Unless it is possible to believe that officials of the legal system can apply legal rules impartially through juridical logic without resort to considerations of social justice or personal gain, then the Rule of Law ideal will wear thin. Consequently western legal theory has become obsessed with the task of demonstrating the apolitical qualities of judicial reasoning and proving how issues of preference and interest play no part in the legal process. In this vein it is claimed that the Supreme Court of the United States adjudicates according to neutral principles of constitutional law,[4] and that French courts merely extrapolate from the Code Napoleon in hard cases rather than deviating from the rules in line with changes in dominant ideology.[5]

Although most legal philosophers and social theorists like Max Weber[6] and Roberto Unger[7] have taken these last two characteristics of modern law – its formal concept of justice and autonomous legal reasoning – to be more or less real phenomena, this position is not shared by Marxists. Their argument is rather that as a result of the ideology of the Rule of Law, legal phenomena are interpreted in a way which is compatible with that doctrine, even if such a description is strained. Indubitably, however, the ideology will affect legal practices and to a considerable extent laws will be created in a form which is designed to comply with these ideals. Marxists can therefore agree with those sceptics of the legal process who doubt whether the qualities of formal justice and autonomous reasoning can constitute a part of a precise description of modern legal systems. Indeed, I argued above from Marxist premises that the autonomy of legal reasoning was an inaccurate description of the judicial process. Instead of legal thought being a discrete, non-instrumental, and rational investigation of justice, it was portrayed as a dialogue with the background dominant ideology on the basis of the formal constraints of coherence and consistency. Similarly, we must doubt the accuracy of the image of law in terms of formal justice in view of the Marxist contention that the source of law and legal developments lies in the ideology of the dominant class. The judge's aim may be to treat like cases alike, but we can be sure that definitions of similarity and difference are determined by criteria supplied by that dominant ideology. Formal justice is not so much hollow justice but another style of class domination.

So, to sum up, the Marxist view of the form of law in modern society is a public announcement which is posited in an accessible medium such as a Code. These features are determined by the function of law in a mode of production which leads to a separation of the State from civil society. In addition, two other qualities of law are widespread as a result of the predominant style of ideological legitimation, namely a reliance upon formal justice and autonomous legal reasoning. All these aspects are reinforced by the background ideology which legitimates the exercise of power, the Rule of Law. Although these characteristics are not entirely accurate descriptions of the form of law, nevertheless they tally with the aspirations of those citizens acting within the legal system.

An important point to notice about this Marxist explanation of the form of modern law is that it avoids attempts to establish direct links between the material base and all aspects of law. On the contrary, it is claimed that distinctive attributes such as formal justice and autonomy of legal reasoning depend upon complex legitimating ideologies, which are themselves derived from political practices within the relatively autonomous state not directly concerned with the capitalist relations of production. Yet at the same time this explanation is plainly compatible with the principles of historical materialism as they have been described above. It has the further merits of escaping the idealist tendencies of Weber's and Unger's explanations of the form of law, and also of eschewing some of the extravagant claims made falsely in the name of Marxism by the commodity exchange theorists who, following their crude materialist orientation, purport to demonstrate that the modern form of law is a direct reflection of practices within the mode of production.

Now that we have found the source of the relative autonomy of the state, and have identified the ideology of the Rule of Law with its implications for perceptions of the legal form, we can return to our original puzzle which was to discover the reason for the failure of the radical strategy of disobedience to law. The appearance of the neutrality of the state undermines any claim that it is an instrument of class oppression. Laws both constitute and emanate from the liberal state, and because of their intimate connection with this structure of power and its ideology of the Rule of Law, they share its attribute of neutrality. Thus breaches of the law are portrayed as violations of rules reached through a set of fair procedures rather than a blow for freedom from domination. A criminal offender is implicitly challenging a system of government which, if the ideology of the Rule of Law is accepted, permits no one person or group to dominate the rest, so the illegal imposition of one's will over everyone else infringes the fair process of government and amounts to an arrogation of power by the dissenter. As a consequence of this interpretation of the liberal system of power the action of a radical against the law is easily distorted into an individual act of deviance against universally accepted norms of behaviour.

On the other hand, the path of reformism through electoral victories falls into a trap by participating in the liberal procedures of government identified with the Rule of Law. Reformism treats legal institutions as neutral and immune from the influence of the dominant class. Occasional proletarian victories which secure welfare legislation tend to confirm this image of neutrality. As a result of these political practices the Hegelian vision of the liberal state comes to be shared by the working class. They interpret it as an impartial arbiter between conflicting interests rather than as a subtle instrument of control and a solution to the problem of the distribution of power within the ruling class. In effect each piece of reformist legislation reaffirms the ideology of the Rule of Law and thus adds to the stability of the system of power found in a capitalist society. It is at this ideological level that reformism serves the purpose of the ruling class by demonstrating the auton-omy of the state. We must also conclude that reformism cannot lead to an increase in class-consciousness, for each piece of legislation is calculated to deny the existence of class domination and to reaffirm the neutrality of the state.

The experience of radical lawyers reveals the antinomies in the reformist approach with peculiar intensity. On the one hand lawyers assume the role of defenders of the fairness and equality of the legal process, so they strive to ensure that poor people have legal advice and representation, and they are quick to criticize the police and the bureacracy when they ignore a person's liberties by making arrests without cause or by searching homes without reasonable grounds for suspecting the presence of incriminating evidence. At the same time, by participating in the machinery of legal justice, the radical lawyer assists the propagation of the ideologies composing the ideal of the Rule of Law. Concern for equal treatment and the preservation of legality are the virtues of liberal society which Marxists are bound to expose as mechanisms which obscure the reality of class domination. Whichever way the lawyer turns, therefore, he is confronted by unsatisfactory choices. Indeed, to be a Marxist and a lawyer promises to be a contradictory or schizoid existence.

The source of the radical's predicament thus lies in the very nature of the legal system in a capitalist society. It is the underlying ideology of the Rule of Law which inspires the liberal system of political power and which frustrates the radical at every turn. Both attempts to capture the law in order to reform it and deliberate violations of law as a form of political protest tend in themselves to raise opportunities for the defenders of the Rule of Law to strengthen its legitimacy as a structure of power in the eyes of the population. But it is precisely through this analysis of the reasons for the radical's failure that the road forward becomes clear. It is the principle of the Rule of Law itself which is the chief obstacle in the path of the development of class-consciousness. As long as such a theory of the system of power remains the dominant interpretation of political practice any counter-ideology which intimates that the liberal state is fundamentally a structure of class domination will be ignored. The broad direction of correct practice for a radical lawyer must be to play a part in demystifying this preponderant ideology of the Rule of Law. How should this task be approached in detail?

It is a battle about definitions of social institutions and how they function. Yet this does not reduce the radical's programme to a war of words. His materialistic understanding of the nature and origins of ideologies points him towards the development of practices on which counter-ideologies can be founded. Theoretical critique must go hand in hand with practices which render the critique meaningful. It cannot be effective if it only occurs in abstractions generated in the halls of academia.

Most practices which are instigated in order to challenge the neutrality of the liberal political order will seek to reveal the class character of the State through conflicts which force the hand of the ruling class. If the latter is induced to impose strict regimes of class rule involving close collaboration between government and the owners of the means of production then the opportunities for fostering class-consciousness will be increased considerably. It is unlikely that practices concerned with law will be deeply involved in this revolutionary strategy except in so far as there may be incidental illegalities. Collective struggles should transcend concern for individual legal rights and justice according to law, for the point is to contest the ideology of the Rule of Law not to uphold it.

There is, however, a limited range of activities by which lawyers may skirmish with the ideology of the Rule of Law. The prevalent belief in the two features of modern law which are natural complements to that ideology can certainly be undermined. The ideal of formal equality in the liberal conception of justice has always provided a prime target for Marxists. Marx himself constantly ridiculed formal equality under the law on the ground that it fails to take into account the enormously disparate circumstances of citizens. He insisted that equal rights only give a right to social inequality.[8] Thus the equal right to own property both ignores and obscures the fact that many citizens own hardly any property at all. Radical criminological studies have also demonstrated that formal legal rights, such as the right to legal representation before a court, permit unequal representation in practice because the poor cannot afford to pay the lawyers, or to exercise other rights granted to them by law.[9]

The autonomy of legal reasoning, the second aspect of the modern form of law derived from the ideology of the Rule of Law, can also be challenged by Marxists, thereby shaking the hold of the Rule of Law on the popular imagination. The task here is to demonstrate the ideological determination of legal rules and doctrine. Any practice or claim which serves to buttress the belief in the autonomy of legal reasoning must be demystified. Suitable targets are presented not only by instrumental legislation or judicial interpretation of statutes in an instrumental fashion in support of the ruling class, but also by fields of law (like Contract with its body of relatively general and abstract principles) which aspire to higher levels of juristic thought but which are open to attack on the ground that legal thought is not autonomous but simply responds to the background dominant ideology. Already critiques of the autonomy of legal thought have penetrated deeply into lawyers' consciousness. Legal philosophers such as Hayek[10] and Unger[11] have remarked on the degeneration of the belief in law as a rational impartial body of rules. Clearly a radical needs to seize this opportunity presented by disillusionment with the autonomy of legal reasoning to propagate the counter-ideology that the liberal state is in a deep structural fashion an instrument of class domination.

This project for radicals should not, of course, degenerate into a claim that all the law simply serves the economic interests of the dominant class. Nothing could be more contrary to the understanding of the principles of historical materialism recounted in this book. To be sure, some pieces of legislation or examples of judicial interpretation may obviously favour a dominant interest group. But in practice the laws of modern society are more subtle in their defence of the social order because of their fidelity to the theoretical neutrality of the state and the ideology of the Rule of Law. Thus the task for a radical is more complex than class instrumentalist theories of law suggest. By an examination of the material origins of laws, a Marxist should reveal that the ideological interpretations of reality contained therein are contingent upon the maintenance of a mode of production which necessarily involves class exploitation. The stage should then be set for the generation of class-consciousness.

So the ideology of the Rule of Law is a central target for Marxist political practice. What is needed is a programme for the demystification of the neutrality of the liberal political order, and its replacement by an appreciation of the class structure of government. The most vital areas for this ideological struggle will occur in practices only tangentially concerned with law, but since the form of law routinely endorses the Rule of Law ideology it merits a Marxist critique. This must be the principal aim of Marxist jurisprudence.

Of course, this conclusion leaves largely untouched the broader dilemma faced by radicals outlined at the beginning of this chapter. The Marxist analysis of the form of law merely demonstrates why both the insurrectionist and the reformist strategy founder in front of an apparently neutral legal system. They encounter a powerful ideology which is directed against an awareness of the presence of class rule, and interaction with the legal system is likely to strengthen rather than to undermine this ideology.

(3) Legality and Liberty

It follows, I think, that the general dilemma faced by many radicals with regard to law must be approached pragmatically. There may be moments when either reformism or insurrection will yield short-term gains for the working class. These benefits must be weighed against the probable consequence of encounters with the legal system – that the foundations of the liberal state are likely to be made more secure against revolutionary action.

In certain cases, however, there will be a relatively clear choice for the radical. Taking the touchstone of Marxist strategy to be the heightening of class-consciousness, it is evident that certain legal conditions increase the opportunities for a working-class movement to gain cohesion. The kinds of rights which will be useful are freedoms to join political associations, to hold meetings and demonstrations, and to disseminate literature. Furthermore, only when there is a powerful labour union organization which can unite the industrial proletariat will there be effective working-class support for such general political liberties. Thus, the first step for revolutionary movements will be to win rights to organize unions in the work-place. Once laws against combinations and strikes have been abolished and legal recognition of the freedom of association for trade unions established, then the way is open for the foundation of working-class organizations which seek political liberties and then finally create a revolutionary working-class movement.

It is thus entirely consistent for Marxist to be suspicious of modern legal systems in general, but at the same time to preserve a strong determination to support fundamental political liberties. Whereas the laws of a liberal democracy obscure the class relations produced by the capitalist mode of production, the elementary rights of political activity serve to ease the path of working-class organizations to establish revolutionary consciousness. There is of course a danger for the radical that these basic liberties will be perceived as ends in themselves rather than as means to achieve the higher goal of transcending bourgeois society. In other words, the existence of liberties to join political associations and to mount effective campaigns may be mistaken for an equal distribution of power and the presence of true freedom. But these equal rights only ensure the continuation of unequal resources of power derived from ownership of the means of production because the formal rights conceal the real relations of class domination. For a radical, the guarantees for free political agitation provided by bourgeois liberties are not the goal of politics but a stepping-stone towards true democracy based on a Communist mode of production.

Yet the dividing line between political liberties which are important for a working-class movement and those which are unnecessary will often be uncertain. At bottom the contrast is between legal rights which merely serve to obscure the structure of class domination, and those which also remove obstructions from the path of a revolutionary movement. This guiding principle marks out some clear cases where reformist and legalistic tactics will be appropriate. For example, in France recently there was a subtle attempt to hamper the right of freedom of association.[12] A government official refused to hand over the documents necessary for an organization to obtain legal capacity to a political party called the 'Association des Amis de la Cause du Peuple' led by Jean-Paul Sartre and Simone de Beauvoir among others. This administrative manœuvre was successfully challenged in the courts on the ground that the official had exceeded his legal powers. In response to the court's ruling, the Government then introduced a Bill into Parliament designed to supply the requisite powers to the official, but this law was held to be invalid in a famous decision of the Conseil Constitutionnel on the ground that the law interfered with freedom of association which was a basic right enshrined in the Declaration of the Rights of Man 1789. In this case there could surely be no doubt that an important political liberty was being infringed. Equally certain is that this right is extremely useful for working-class organizations so it had to be defended vigorously. The application of the guiding principle is not, however, always so readily apparent.

How, for instance, should a Marxist view incursions against the right to a fair trial? A strand of the ideology of the Rule of Law is that the law should be applied to each citizen without partiality. Thus there will be an infringement of the principle if the judge or jury were so biased as to be predisposed to find the accused guilty before hearing the evidence or even despite the proven facts. Should the radical be concerned if the powerful always escape scot-free, or those tarnished by the police with the accusation of holding radical views are condemned and dealt with severely by a court without there being sufficient evidence to support a conviction? Is the right to a fair trial so closely tied to the organization of working-class solidarity that it is a freedom which is a vital part of the struggle? If it could be successfully shown that there had been a departure from the principles of the Rule of Law then certainly considerable embarrassment would be experienced by those persons responsible. A widespread campaign to demonstrate that the commitment of the ruling group to the Rule of Law was a sham might even topple the powerful and ensure their replacement by politicians more faithful to the spirit of the liberal state. But it is evident that such criticism of government action to preserve the reality of the right to a fair trial is peripheral to the main course of a radical programme promoting working-class consciousness. It is really more directed towards upholding the Rule of Law than revealing the class structure of a capitalist society. There is a danger that continual discussion of petty incursions of civil liberties found in the criminal process will raise those rights infringed to the status of ends rather than means. In other words, the ideology of the impartiality of criminal justice might become the goal of radical movements when it should only constitute a side-show, and the class struggle would degenerate into a defence of the Rule of Law.

Although this pragmatic approach to the legal system has been the predominant theme within the Marxist tradition, over recent years it has been seriously questioned. A degree of uneasiness is felt over the reduction of concern for bourgeois political liberties and the principle of legality in government action to the level of treating them as means towards the revolutionary goal to be used and defended whenever appropriate, rather than desirable ends in themselves. It is wondered whether or not there may be some intrinsic value to individual rights and the requirement that the state apparatus be constrained by its own rules.

The reason for this ambivalence is not hard to find. Marxists are sensitive to the fact that they are often associated with dictatorial and totalitarian systems of government as a consequence of Stalin's ruthless exercise of power in the USSR under the banner of Communism. Of course, the horrors of that dictatorship were no part of the original vision of Communism, yet the popular association of that form of government with Marxism has persisted. To protect themselves from allegations of totalitarianism, Marxists have acknowledged the effectiveness of the principle of legality in taming the exercise of official power, they have admitted that formal equality of political rights is better than status differentation, and E. P. Thompson even goes so far as to ascribe an intrinsic value to the goal of ensuring the legality of government action.[13] This last position threatens, of course, to slide into a wholesale acceptance of the Rule of Law.

Is there any inconsistency in valuing on the one hand the principle of legality in government action and political rights, and on the other hand seeking to undermine the ideology of the Rule of Law? Of course there is a contradiction within modern Marxism here. No amount of casuistry can conceal the point that the ideology of the Rule of Law is behind the concern for legality and liberty. The principle of legality is enmeshed in practices associated with the Rule of Law, and some philosophers (wrongly, I think) have limited the latter idea to a concern for the legality of government action.[14] Certainly the principle of legality is implicit in the concept of the sovereignty of law and the ideal of impartial enforcement of rules, which constitute important elements in my broad conception of the Rule of Law. Similarly, though less distinctly and only partially, the concern for political liberties is inspired by the idea of an autonomous state where every citizen has an equal opportunity to gain access to political power. The preservation of such liberties apparently ensures the neutrality of the state between conflicting groups, and prevents any one group from gaining a monopoly of power. The ideal of the Rule of Law is a linchpin in this image of power relations. Marxists are therefore inconsistent when they both uphold the virtues of legality and liberty and at the same time criticize the Rule of Law.

Yet this contradiction persistently reappears in Marxist writings about law and state. Is there some independent ground for valuing legality and liberty even though there is a commitment to the overthrow of the whole system of class domination which those principles obscure? Some might argue that bourgeois formal freedom is better than no liberty at all, and for that reason legality and liberty should be defended. But it is unclear that this argument is available to Marxists.

Indeed, the status of moral judgments ventured by Marxists is perplexing.[15] The problem is to establish standards which are distinctively Marxist. Obviously any evaluation of institutions according to conventional morality would be impermissible because those criteria embody the dominant ideology including the Rule of Law, the very principles which Marxists are attempting to subvert. Marx often used this approach to expose hypocrisy within the relatively autonomous state, but he was surely not intending to condone those moral standards. There seem to be only two possible ways in which Marxists might ascribe moral worth to the pursuit of particular political principles such as legality and liberty. The first is to assess institutions and policies according to a functional test which considers to what extent they hasten progress towards a revolution. The second uses the theory of alienation, and evaluates institutional arrangements and political principles in the light of Man's true nature to discover whether freedom for self-affirmation through labour is permitted or encouraged by them. Neither of these approaches to moral judgment can, however, support a blanket concern for legality and liberty.

First, if a Marxist chooses to assess the goodness of action in a functional or purposive manner according to the criterion of the development of revolutionary class-consciousness, then, because it is unlikely that concern for legality or liberty in general (as opposed to specific instances as in the case of the 'Association des Amis de la Cause du Peuple') will foster class-consciousness, it cannot be argued that these principles have intrinsic merit. Alternatively, if a Marxist values institutional arrangements according to the degree to which they approximate to the goal of history, an unalienated society, then it is far from clear whether the relatively autonomous state governed according to the Rule of Law is closer in structure than any previous social formation to the institutional arrangements necessary for true freedom, or whether modern society represents on the contrary the quintessence of an alienated existence. On balance, the relatively autonomous state appears to promote alienation rather than provide the necessary conditions for self-affirmation through labour because it helps to preserve the capitalist mode of production. Thus on the basis of either of these two standards for assessing the moral worth of a political principle according to Marxist tenets, a concern for legality and liberty is unlikely to score very high.

There is an unresolved contradiction in the Marxist position in so far as it includes a blanket concern for legality and liberty as well as an attack on the Rule of Law. Support for fundamental political liberties through legal mechanisms may be permitted because of the possible instrumental gains to the working-class movement. But any wider belief in the intrinsic merit of preserving the legality of government action and defending individual rights makes the mistake of taking the ideology of the Rule of Law at face value. The ideological function of the modern legal system in obscuring class domination renders an undiscriminating pursuit of the principle of legality inconsistent with Marxism.

Notes

Chapter 1. The Marxist Approach to Law

(1) e.g. Kelsen, H. *The Communist Theory of Law* (Stevens, London, 1955); Hayek, F. A. *The Constitution of Liberty* (Routledge and Kegan Paul, London, 1960) pp. 239–40.

(2) Collections of this literature in translation are found in Babb, H. W. and Hazard, H. (eds.) *Soviet Legal Philosophy* (Harvard University Press, Cambridge, Mass., 1951); Jaworskyj, M. (ed.) *Soviet Political Thought* (Johns Hopkins University Press, Baltimore, 1967); and *Soviet Law and Government* (International Arts and Sciences Press, New York).

(3) Renner, K. *The Institutions of Private Law and their Social Functions*. ed. Kahn-Freund, O. (Routledge and Kegan Paul, London, 1949).

(4) Pashukanis, E. B. *Law and Marxism*. ed. Arthur, C. J. (Ink Links, London, 1978).

(5) Cain, M. and Hunt, A. *Marx and Engels on Law* (Academic Press, London, 1979).

(6) Hart, H. L. A. *The Concept of Law* (Oxford, 1961) p. 189 ff.

(7) Ibid. p. 89 ff.

(8) e.g. Dworkin, R. M. *Taking Rights Seriously* (Duckworth, London, 1979) ch. 11; Finnis, J. *Natural Law and Natural Rights* (Oxford, 1980) Ch. X; Fuller, L. L. *The Morality of Law* (Yale, 2nd ed., 1969) Ch. 2; Raz, J. *The Authority of Law* (Oxford, 1979) Ch. 11.

Chapter 2. Law as an Instrument of Class Oppression

(1) Marx, K. 'Preface to a Contribution to the Critique of Political Economy', in *Early Writings*. ed. Colletti, L. (Penguin/NLR, 1975) p. 424.

(2) Marx, K. and Engels, F. *The German Ideology*. Part I, ed. Arthur, C. J. (Lawrence and Wishart, London, 1970).

(3) See Marx, K. *Capital*, Vol. 1 (Penguin/New Left Review, 1976) p. 883.

(4) Ibid. Chs. 10, 15(3), (9).

(5) Engels, F. 'Ludwig Feuerbach and the End of Classical German Philosophy', in Karl Marx and Frederick Engels, *Selected Works* (International Publishers, New York, 1968) p. 626 ff.; Engels, F. letter to C. Schmidt, 27 October 1890, in ibid. p. 694.

(6) Engels, F. letter to J. Block, 21 Sept. 1890, in ibid. p. 692.

(7) Pashukanis, E. B. *Law and Marxism* (Ink Links, London, 1978) pp. 91, 96, 167.

(8) See Marx, K. *Capital* Penguin/NLR, (1976) Vol. I, p. 178; Kinsey, R. 'Marxism and the law: Preliminary Analyses' (1978) 5 *British Jour. of Law and Society* 202.

(9) Cohen, G. A. *Karl Marx's Theory of History: A Defence* (Oxford, 1978).

(10) Lenin, V. I. *The State and Revolution* (Foreign Languages Press, Peking, 1976).

(11) See Balbus, I. D. *The Dialectics of Legal Repression* (Russell Sage, New York, 1973).

Chapter 3. Ideology and Law

(1) Marx, K. 'Preface to a Contribution to the Critique of Political Economy', in *Early Writings*. ed. Colletti, L. (Penguin/NLR, 1975) p. 424.

(2) See Marx, K. 'Theses on Feuerbach', in *Early Writings*. p. 421; and Taylor, C. *Marxism and Empiricism*. in Williams, B. and Montefiore, A. (eds.) *British Analytical Philosophy* (Routledge and Kegan Paul, London, 1966) Ch. 10.

(3) c.f. Webb, S. and Webb. B. *The History of Trade Unionism* (Longmans, London, 1920) p. 70 ff.

(4) Thompson, E. P. *The Poverty of Theory* (Merlin Press, London, 1978).

(5) Anderson, P. *Arguments Within English Marxism* (Verso, London, 1980) Ch. 1.

(6) Marx, K. *Capital*, Vol. 1 (Penguin/New Left Review, 1976) pp. 392–5.

(7) Hay, D. Property, 'Authority and the Criminal Law', in Hay, D., Linebaugh, P., and Thompson, E. P. *Albion's Fatal Tree* (Allen Lane, London, 1975).

(8) Poulantzas, N. *Political Power and Social Classes* (New Left Books and Sheed & Ward, London, 1975) p. 193, and p. 255 ff.; Poulantzas, N., 'The Capitalist State: A reply to Miliband and Laclau', 95 *New Left Review* 63 (1976); Miliband, R. *Marxism and Politics* (Oxford, 1977) Ch. IV, p. 83 ff.

(9) Gramsci, A. *Selections from Prison Notebooks* (Lawrence and Wishart, London, 1971), pp. 195–6, and 246–7.

(10) Althusser, L. 'Ideology and Ideological State Apparatuses', in *Lenin and Philosophy and Other Essays* (New Left Books, London, 1971) pp. 121–73; see also: Sumner, C. *Reading Ideologies* (Academic Press, London, 1979) Chs. 1, 2, 6; Hirst, P. *On Law and Ideology* (Macmillan, London, 1979), Chs. 2, 3.

(11) Althusser, L. *For Marx* (New Left Books, London, 1977) p. 114.

(12) Renner, K. *The Institutions of Private Law and Their Social Functions* ed. Kahn-Freund, O. (Routledge and Kegan Paul, London, 1949).

(13) Law Reform (Miscellaneous Provisions) Act, 1970.

(14) Sugarman, D. *Legality, Ideology and the State* (Academic Press, London, 1983), p. 125.

(15) Marx, K. *Capital.* Vol. 1 (Penguin/New Left Review, 1976) Ch. 28; Harring, S. L. 'Class Conflict and the Suppression of Tramps in Buffalo, 1892–1894', 11 *Law & Society Review* (1977) p. 873.

(16) Poulantzas, N. *Political Power and Social Classes*, p. 84.

(17) Horwitz, M. J. *The Transformation of American Law 1780–1860* (Harvard, Cambridge, Mass., 1977) pp. 256–9.

(18) Fox, A. *Beyond Contract: Work, Power and Trust Relations* (Faber, London, 1974) Ch. 4.

(19) Unger, R. M. *Law in Modern Society* (Free Press, New York, 1976) pp. 52–3.

(20) MacCormick, N. *Legal Reasoning and Legal Theory* (Oxford, 1978).

(21) Dworkin, R. M. *Taking Rights Seriously* (Duckworth, London, 1978).

(22) Engels, F. letter to C. Schmidt, 27 Oct. 1890, in Karl Marx and Frederick Engels, *Selected Works* (International Publishers, New York, 1968) p. 694.

(23) Thompson, E. P. *The Poverty of Theory* (Merlin Press, London, 1978) p. 288.

(24) Cain, M. and Hunt, A. *Marx and Engels on Law* (Academic Press, London, 1979) p. 50; Cotterrell, R., 'The Development of Capitalism and the Formalisation of Contract Law', in Fryer, B., Hunt, A., McBarnet, D., and Moorhouse, B., *Law, State and Society* (Croom Helm, London, 1981) p. 58.

(25) Cain, M. and Hunt, A. op. cit. p. 109.

(26) Rheinstein, M. (ed.) *Max Weber on Law in Economy and Society* (Simon & Schuster, New York, 1954) p. 131 ff.; Tigar, M. E. and Levy, M. R. *Law and the Rise of Capitalism* (Monthly Review Press, London, 1977).

(27) e.g. Hepburn, J. R. *Social Control and the Legal Order: Legitimated Repression in a Capitalist State,* Contemporary Crises, 1 (1977) pp. 77–90.

Chapter 4. Base and Superstructure

(1) Williams, R. *Marxism and Literature* (Oxford, 1977) pp. 75–82; Thompson, E. P. 'Folklore, Anthropology, and Social History', *Indian Historical Review* (1977) 247–66; Cain, M. and Hunt, A. *Marx and Engels on Law* (Academic Press, London, 1979) pp. 48–51; Thompson, E. P. *The Poverty of Theory* (Merlin, London, 1978) p. 288.

(2) Plamenatz, J. *German Marxism and Russian Communism* (Longmans, London, 1954) Ch. 2; Plamenatz, J. *Man and Society.* Vol. 2 (Longmans, London, 1963) p. 280 ff.

(3) e.g. Winch, P. *The Idea of Social Science* (London, Routledge and Kegan Paul, 1958) but also exchange theory, role theory, and types of interaction theory.

(4) Taylor, J. O. *The Law Affecting River Pollution* (Green & Son, Edinburgh, 1928).

(5) Cohen, G. A. *Karl Marx's Theory of History: A Defence* (Oxford, 1978) Ch. VIII.

(6) Plamenatz, *Man and Society.* Vol. 2, p. 282 ff.

(7) Hart, H. L. A. *The Concept of Law* (Oxford, 1961) pp. 86–8.

(8) Gramsci, A. *Selections from the Prison Notebooks.* pp. 195–6.

Chapter 5. The Prognosis for Law

(1) e.g. Lloyd, D. *Introduction to Jurisprudence* (Stevens, London, 1979) Ch. 10.

(2) See Cohen, G. A. *Karl Marx's Theory of History: A Defence* (Oxford, 1978) Ch. V.

(3) e.g. Marx, K. 'The Trial of the Rhineland District Committee of Democrats', in Fernbach D. (ed.) *The Revolutions of 1848* (Penguin/NLR 1973): 'Society is not founded upon the law; that is a legal fiction. On the contrary, the law must be founded upon society . . .'

(4) Pashukanis, E. B. *Law and Marxism*, Ch. 3.

(5) Balbus, I. D. 'Commodity Form and Legal Form', in Reasons, C. E. and Rich, R. M. *The Sociology of Law* (Butterworths, Toronto, 1978) pp. 83-5.

(6) e.g. Poulantzas, N. *Nature des choses et droit* (LGDJ, Paris, 1965).

(7) Engels, F. *Anti-Dühring* (Foreign Languages Press, Peking, 1976) Part III, Ch. 2.

(8) Lenin, V. I. *The State and Revolution* (Foreign Languages Press, Peking, 1976) Chs. I & V.

(9) Ibid. p. 110.

(10) Pashukanis, E. B. *Law and Marxism*.

(11) Ibid. Editor's introduction, pp. 15-16.

(12) Tönnies, F. *Community and Association* (Gemeinschaft und Gesellschaft) translated and supplemented by Loomis, C. P. V. (London, 1955).

(13) Nozick, R. *Anarchy, State, and Utopia* (Blackwell, Oxford, 1974).

(14) Hart, H. L. A. *The Concept of Law* (Oxford, 1961) Ch. IX (2).

(15) Marx, K. 'Economic and Philosophical Manuscripts', in *Early Writings*. ed. Colletti, L. (Penguin/NLB, 1975) pp. 322-34.

(16) Althusser, L. *For Marx* (New Left Books, London, 1977) Ch. 7.

Chapter 6. Class Struggle and the Rule of Law

(1) Marx, K. 'Critique of Hegel's Doctrine of the State', in *Early Writings*. ed. Colletti, L. (Penguin/NLR 1975) pp. 57-198.

(2) For a survey see: Jessop, B. 'Recent Theories of the Capitalist State', 1 *Cambridge Jour. of Economics* 353 (1977).

(3) Wedderburn, K. W. *The Worker and the Law* (2nd ed.) (Penguin, 1971) pp. 75-6.

(4) Wechsler, 'Towards Neutral Principles in Constitutional Law', 73 *Harv. LR* 1 (1959). Dworkin, R. M. *Taking Rights Seriously* (Duckworth, London, 1978) Ch. 4.

(5) Aubry, C. and Rau, C. *Cours de droit civil français* (ed. 4, 1869 Paris) s. 40. C.f. Dawson, J. P: *The Oracles of the Law* (Ann Arbor, Michigan, 1968) pp. 400-31.

(6) Weber, M. *On Law in Economy and Society*. ed. Rheinstein, M. (Simon & Schuster, New York, 1954) Ch. IV.

(7) Unger, R. M. *Law in Modern Society*. pp. 52-8.

(8) Marx, K. 'Critique of the Gotha Programme', in Karl Marx and Frederick Engels, *Selected Works* (International Publishers, New York, 1968) pp. 315-35.

(9) e.g. Carlin, J. E. and Howard, J. 'Legal Representation and Class Justice', 12 *UCLA LR* 381 (1965).

(10) Hayek, F. A. *The Constitution of Liberty* (Routledge and Kegan Paul, London, 1960) Ch. 15.

(11) Unger, R. M. op cit. pp. 193-200.

(12) D 1972, 685; JCP 1971, II, 16832; AJ 1971, 537, note Rivero; cf Nicholas, 'Fundamental Rights and Judicial Review in France' (1978) *Public Law* 82, 155.

(13) Thompson, E. P. *Whigs and Hunters: The Origin of the Black Act* (Allen Lane, 1975) p. 266.

(14) e.g. Raz, J. *The Authority of Law* (Oxford, 1979) Ch. 11.

(15) Cf Bottomore, T. (ed.) *Modern Interpretations of Marx* (Blackwell, Oxford, 1981); Kamenka, E. *Marxism and Ethics* (Macmillan, London, 1969).

Select Bibliography

Chapter 1. The Marxist Approach to Law

(1) What is Marxism?

ANDERSON, P. *Considerations of Western Marxism*, (NLR, London, 1976).

BOTTOMORE, T. (ed.) *Modern Interpretations of Marx* (Blackwell, Oxford, 1981).

COLLETTI, L. *From Rousseau to Lenin* (New Left Books, London, 1973).

KOLAKOWSKI, L. *Main Currents of Marxism* (3 Vols., Oxford, 1978).

LICHTHEIM, G. *Marxism* (Routledge and Kegan Paul, London, 1964).

McLELLAN, D. *Karl Marx, His Life and Thought* (Paladin, St. Albans, 1973).

SINGER, P. *Marx* (Oxford, 1980).

WOOD, A. *Karl Marx* (Routledge and Kegan Paul, London, 1981).

(2) Is there a Marxist Theory of Law?

BALBUS, I. D. 'Commodity Form and Legal Form', *Law and Society Review*, Vol. 11 (1977) 571–88; also in REASONS, C. E. and RICH, R. M. *The Sociology of Law* (Butterworths, Toronto, 1978).

BRIMO, A. *Les Grands Courants de la philosophie du droit et de l'état* (Pedone, Paris 3rd ed. 1978).

CAIN, M. and HUNT, A. *Marx and Engels on Law* (Academic Press, London, 1979).

CHKHIKVADZE, V. *The State, Democracy and Legality in the USSR. Lenin's Ideas Today* (Progress, Moscow, 1972).

EDELMAN, B. *Ownership of the Image* (Routledge and Kegan Paul, London, 1979).

FRASER, A. 'The Legal Theory We Need Now', *Socialist Review* (1978). Nos. 40–1 (Vol. 8, Nos. 4–5) p. 147.

HIRST, P. Q. 'Marx and Engels on law, crime and morality', in TAYLOR, I., WALTON, P., and YOUNG, J. (Eds.) *Critical Criminology* (Routledge and Kegan Paul, London, 1975).

HUNT, A. 'Law, State and Class Struggle', *Marxism Today*, Vol. 20 (1976) pp. 178–87.

—— 'Marxism and the Analysis of Law', in *Sociological Approaches to Law*, ed. PODGÓRECKI, A., and WHEELAN, C. J. (Croom Helm, London, 1981).

KINSEY, R. 'Marxism and the Law: Preliminary Analyses' (1978) 5 *British Journal of Law and Society* 202.

KLARE, K. 'Law-Making as Praxis', *Telos* (Summer, 1979) 123.

LLOYD, D. and FREEMAN, M. D. A. (eds.) *Introduction to Jurisprudence* (Stevens, London, 1979) Ch. 10.

MIAILLE, M. *Une Introduction critique au droit* (François Maspero, Paris, 1977).

PASHUKANIS, E. B. *Law and Marxism* ed. ARTHUR, C. J. (Ink Links, London. 1978).

PHILLIPS, P. *Marx and Engels on Law and Laws* (Martin Robertson, Oxford, 1980).

RENNER, K. *The Institutions of Private Law and their Social Functions,* ed. KAHN-FREUND, O. (Routledge and Kegan Paul, London, 1949).

SZABO, I. *Les Fondements de la Théorie du Droit* (Akademiai Kiadó, Budapest, 1973).

TUSHNET, M. A. 'A Marxist Analysis of American Law', *Marxist Perspectives,* No. 1 (Spring, 1978).

WEYL, N. and R. *La Part du Droit dans la réalité et dans l'action* (Editions Sociales, Paris, 1968).

Chapter 2. Law as an Instrument of Class Oppression

(1) Elements of Historical Materialism

ANDERSON, P. *Arguments Within English Marxism* (Verso, London, 1980) Chs. 2, 3.

COHEN, G. A. *Karl Marx's Theory of History: A Defence* (Oxford, 1978).

ENGELS, F. letter to J. Bloch, 21 Sept. 1890, in Karl Marx and Frederick Engels, *Selected Works* (International Publishers, New York, 1968) p. 692.

MARX, K. and ENGELS, F. *The German Ideology,* Part 1, ed. ARTHUR, C. J. (Lawrence and Wishart, 1970).

—— 'Preface to a Contribution to the Critique of Political Economy', in *Early Writings,* ed. COLLETTI, L. (Penguin/NLR 1975) p. 424.

—— and ENGELS, F. 'Manifesto of the Communist Party', in *The Revolutions of 1848* ed. FERNBACH, D. (Penguin/NLR 1973).

Chapter 3. Ideology and Law

(1) The Marxist Theory of Ideology

AVINERI, S. *The Social and Political Thought of Karl Marx* (Cambridge, 1968) Ch. 3.

HIRST, P. *On Law and Ideology* (Macmillan, London, 1979).

LARRAIN, J. *The Concept of Ideology* (Hutchinson, London, 1979) Ch. 2.

MARX, K. and ENGELS, F. *The German Ideology,* Part 1.

PLAMENATZ, J. *Man and Society,* Vol. 2 (Longman, London, 1963) pp. 323–50.

SUMNER, C. *Reading Ideologies* (Academic Press, London, 1979).

TAYLOR, C. 'Marxism and Empiricism', in WILLIAMS, B. and MONTEFIORE, A. (eds.) *British Analytical Philosophy* (Routledge and Kegan Paul, London, 1966) Ch. 10.

WILLIAMS, R. *Marxism and Literature* (Oxford, 1977) pp. 55–71.

(2) Class Reductionism

ALTHUSSER, L. *For Marx* (New Left Books, London, 1977) Ch. 3.

—— *Lenin and Philosophy* (New Left Books, London, 1971).

BEIRNE, P. *Fair Rent and Legal Fiction* (Macmillan, London, 1977).

—— 'Empiricism and the Critique of Marxism on Law and Crime', *Social Problems*, Vol. 26, No. 4 (1979) 373.

CROUCH, C. 'The State, Capital and Liberal Democracy', in CROUCH, C. (ed.) *State and Economy in Contemporary Capitalism* (Croom Helm, London, 1979).

EORSI, G. *Comparative Civil (Private) Law* (Akamediai Kiado, Budapest, 1979), Introduction and Ch. 9.

FEMIA, J. 'Hegemony and Consciousness in the Thought of Antonio Gramsci', 23 *Pol. Studies* 29 (1975).

GRAMSCI, A. *Selections from the Prison Notebooks* (Lawrence and Wishart, London, 1971).

HAY, D. 'Property, Authority and the Criminal Law', in HAY, D., LINEBAUGH. P., and THOMPSON, E. P., *Albion's Fatal Tree* (Allen Lane, London, 1975).

HEPBURN, J. R. 'Social Control and the Legal Order: Legitimated Repression in a Capitalist State', *Contemporary Crises*, 1 (1977) pp. 77–90.

MARX, K. *Capital*, Vol. 1 (Penguin, New Left Review, 1976) Chs. 10, 27, 28.

MILIBAND, R. *Marxism and Politics* (Oxford, 1977) Chs. III and IV.

RENNER, K. *The Institutions of Private Law and their Social Functions*. ed. KAHN-FREUND, O. (Routledge and Kegan Paul, London, 1949).

WILLIAMS, R. *Marxism and Literature* (Oxford, 1977) pp. 108–20.

(3) The Autonomy of Legal Thought

ENGELS, F. letter to C. Schmidt, 27 Oct. 1890, in Karl Marx and Frederick Engels, *Selected Works* (International Publishers, New York, 1968) p. 694.

GRIFFITH, J. A. G. *The Politics of the Judiciary* (Fontana, 1977).

MILIBAND, R. *The State in Capitalist Society* (Quartet, London, 1973) pp. 124–30.

Chapter 4. Base and Superstructure

ANDERSON, P. *Lineages of the Absolutist State* (New Left Books, 1974) pp. 401–3.

COHEN, G. A. *Karl Marx's Theory of History: A Defence* (Oxford, 1978).

PLAMENATZ, J. *Man and Society*, Vol. 2 (Longman, London, 1963) pp. 274–93.

—— *German Marxism and Russian Communism* (Longmans, London, 1954) Ch. 2.
THOMPSON, E. P. *Whigs and Hunters: The Origins of the Black Act* (Allen Lane, 1975) pp. 258–66.
WILLIAMS, R. *Marxism and Literature* (Oxford, 1977) pp. 75–94.

Chapter 5. The Prognosis for Law

(1) Fetishism of Law

MAILLE, M. *Une Introduction critique au droit* (François Maspero, Paris, 1977) pp. 94–118.
MARX, K. *Capital,* Vol. 1 (Penguin, New Left Review, 1976) Ch. 1(4).
TOUMANOV, V. *Pensée juridique bourgeoise contemporaine* (Progress, Moscow, 1974) Ch. 1.

(2) The Withering Away of Law

BERMAN, H. J. *Justice in the USSR* (Harvard, 1963).
COTTERELL, R. 'Commodity Form and Legal Form', *Ideology and Consciousness* (1976) No. 6, 111.
ENGELS, F. *Anti-Dühring* (Foreign Languages Press, Peking, 1976) Part III.
FULLER, L. L. 'Pashukanis and Vyshinsky: A Study in the Development of Marxian Legal Theory', 47 *Michigan Law Review* 1159 (1949).
KAMENKA, E. and TAY, A. 'The Life and After Life of a Bolshevik Jurist', *Problems of Communism* (1970) Part 1, p. 72.
LENIN, V. I. *The State and Revolution* (Foreign Languages Press, Peking, 1976).
PASHUKANIS, E. B. *Law and Marxism,* ed. ARTHUR, C. J. (Ink Links, London, 1978).
PLAMENATZ, J. *Man and Society,* Vol. 2 (Longman, London, 1963) pp. 351–87.
WARRINGTON, R. 'Pashukanis and the Commodity Form Theory', *International Journal of the Sociology of Law* (1981), 9, pp. 1–22.

(3) Human Nature

ALTHUSSER, L. *For Marx* (New Left Books, London, 1977) Ch. 7.
KAMENKA, E. *Marxism and Ethics* (Macmillan, London, 1969).
LUKES, S. 'Alienation and Anomie', in LASLETT, P. and RUNCIMAN, W. G. (eds.) *Philosophy, Politics and Society,* 3rd Series (Oxford, 1967) Ch. 6.
MARX, K. 'Economic and Philosophical Manuscripts', in *Early Writings* ed. COLLETTI, L. (Penguin/NLB 1975) pp. 322–34.
PLAMENATZ, J. *Karl Marx's Philosophy of Man* (Oxford, 1975).
WOOD, A. *Karl Marx* (Routledge and Kegan Paul, London, 1981) Part 1.

Chapter 6. Class Struggle and the Rule of Law

(1) The Radical's Predicament

AVINERI, S. *The Social and Political Thought of Karl Marx* (Cambridge, 1968), Ch. 5.

BANKOWSKI, Z. and MUNGHAM, G. *Images of Law* (Routledge and Kegan Paul, London, 1976).

HABERMAS, J. *Toward a Rational Society* (Heinemann, London, 1971).

LIVINGSTONE, A. 'Reflections on the Role of the Radical Lawyer Today', 1 *Law and State* 1 (1977).

MARCUSE, H. *An Essay on Liberation* (Penguin, 1969).

MILIBAND, R. *Marxism and Politics* (Oxford, 1977) Ch. 6.

WARRINGTON, R. 'Law – its Image or its reality', *City of London Law Review* (1977) 29.

(2) The Form of Law

AVINERI, S. op. cit. Ch. 1.

BALBUS, I. D. *The Dialectics of Legal Repression* (Russell Sage, New York, 1973) Ch. 1.

BLANKE, B., JURGENS, U., and KASTENDICK, H. 'On the Current Marxist Discussion on the analysis of Form and Function of the Bourgeois State', in HOLLOWAY, J., PICCIOTTO, S. (eds.) *State and Capital: A Marxist Debate* (Edward Arnold, 1978).

CARLIN, J. E., and HOWARD, J. 'Legal Representation and class justice', 12 *UCLA Law Rev.* 381 (1965).

FINE, B., KINSEY, R., LEA, J., PICCIOTTO, S., and YOUNG, J. (eds.) *Capitalism and the Rule of Law* (Hutchinson, London, 1979) Chs. 1, 2, 3, 11.

HAYEK, F. A. *The Constitution of Liberty* (Routledge and Kegan Paul, London, 1960).

HOLLOWAY, J., PICCIOTTO, S. *State and Capital: A Marxist Debate* (Edward Arnold, 1978) Ch. 1.

HORWITZ, M. J. 'The Rule of Law: An Unqualified Human Good?' 86 *Yale L. J.* 561–6 (1977).

JESSOP, B. 'Recent Theories of the Capitalist State', 1 *Cambridge Jour. of Economics* 353 (1977).

MARX, K. 'Critique of Hegel's Doctrine of the State', in *Early Writings*, ed. COLLETTI, L. (Penguin/NLR 1975).

MARX, K. 'Critique of the Gotha Programme', in *Karl Marx and Frederick Engels, Selected Works* (International Publishers, New York, 1968) pp. 315–35.

NONET, P. and SELZNICK, P. *Law and Society in Transition: Toward Responsive Law* (Harper, New York, 1978).

POULANTZAS, N. *Nature des choses et droit* (LGDJ, Paris, 1965) pp. 251–87.

—— *Political Power and Social Classes* (Verso, London, 1978).

—— *State Power Socialism* (Verso, London, 1980) pp. 76–92.

QUINNEY, R. 'The Ideology of Law: Notes for a Radical Alternative to Legal Oppression', *Issues in Criminology* 7(1) (1972) 1–35; in REASONS, C. E. and RICH, R. M. *The Sociology of Law* (Butterworths, Toronto, 1978).

RAZ, J. *The Authority of Law* (Oxford, 1979) Ch. 11.

UNGER, R. M. *Law in Modern Society* (Free Press, New York, 1976).

(3) Legality and Liberty

ANDERSON, P. *Arguments within English Marxism* (Verso, London, 1980) pp. 197–207.

CAIN, M. 'Optimism, Law and the State: A plea for the possibility of politics' (1977), *European Yearbook in Law and Sociology*, 20–41.

LUKACS, G. *History and Class Consciousness* (Merlin, London, 1971) pp. 256–71.

MARX, K. 'The Trial of the Rhineland District Committee of Democrats, Speech by Karl Marx in his own Defence', in *The Revolutions of 1848*, ed. FERNBACH, D. (Penguin/NLR 1973) p. 245.

THOMPSON, E. P. *Whigs and Hunters: The Origin of the Black Act* (Allen Lane, 1975) pp. 258–66.

—— 'The State versus its "enemies" ', *New Society*, 19 Oct. 1978, pp. 127–30.

Index

OXFORD

MORE OXFORD PAPERBACKS

Details of a selection of other books follow. A complete list of Oxford Paperbacks, including The World's Classics, Twentieth-Century Classics, OPUS, Past Masters, Oxford Authors, Oxford Shakespeare, and Oxford Paperback Reference, is available in the UK from the General Publicity Department, Oxford University Press (JH), Walton Street, Oxford, OX2 6DP.

In the USA, complete lists are available from the Paperbacks Marketing Manager, Oxford University Press, 200 Madison Avenue, New York, NY 10016.

Oxford Paperbacks are available from all good bookshops. In case of difficulty, please order direct from Oxford University Press Bookshop, 116 High Street, Oxford, Freepost, OX1 4BR, enclosing full payment. Please add 10% of published price for postage and packing.

MARXISM AND ANTHROPOLOGY

Maurice Bloch

Praised for it's 'clear-headedness and common sense' (*London Review of Books*), this book is an introduction to the uses made of anthropology by Marx and Engels, and the uses made of Marxism by anthropologists.

'this is an excellent introduction to the subject, unique and indispensable' Ronald Frankenberg, *Sociology*

Marxist Introductions

MARXISM AND PHILOSOPHY

Alex Callinicos

Marxism began with the repudiation of philosophy. Marx declared: 'The philosophers have only *interpreted* the world in various ways; the point is to *change* it.' Yet Marxists have often resorted to philosophical modes of reasoning, and Western Marxism has recently been more concerned with philosophy than with empirical research or political activity.

This book explores the ambivalent attitude of Marxism to philosophy, starting with an examination of the Marxist view of Hegel. Alex Callinicos goes on to contrast the German classical idealism, from which Marxist philosophy stems, with the very different tradition of analytical philosophy prevalent among English-speaking philosophers.

Marxist Introductions

MARXISM AND POLITICS

Ralph Miliband

Neither Marx nor any of his successors sought to define an overall theory of the nature of their political views. Professor Miliband has reconstructed from a wide range of material the main elements of the political theory and actual politics which are specific to Marxism. In so doing he highlights some of the problems left unresolved by earlier Marxists and discusses some pertinent questions of central importance to the politics of the twentieth century.

Marxist Introductions

MARXISM AND LITERATURE

Raymond Williams

Professor Williams analyses previous contributions to a Marxist theory of literature from Marx himself to Lukács, Althusser, and Goldmann, and develops his own approach by outlining a theory of 'cultural materialism' which integrates Marxist theories of language with Marxist theories of literature. The book concludes with a re-examination of the problems of alignment and commitment, and with a discussion of creative practice both in individual authors and in wider social groups.

Marxist Introductions

MARX'S SOCIAL THEORY

Terrell Carver

Why has Marx had such a wide-ranging impact on our intellectual and political life? Terrell Carver presents a new analysis of what Marx called the 'guiding thread' of his studies, which is set out in his 1859 preface *A Critique of Political Economy*, together with an important autobiographical sketch, which the author reanalyses in this book. He argues that Marx's 'production theory of society and social change' is analogous to Darwin's work in a hitherto unnoticed way and is just as scientific. He assesses the central difficulties encountered by the theory, and shows that it sprang from a desire not simply to interpret the world, but to change it.

Marxist Introductions

MAIN CURRENTS OF MARXISM

Its Origins, Growth, and Dissolution

1. The Founders: 2. The Golden Age: 3. The Breakdown

Leszek Kolakowski

Translated by P. S. Falla

Leszek Kolakowski modestly described his three-volume history of Marxism, first published in 1978, as a 'historical manual', a collection of 'the principal facts that are likely to be of use to anyone seeking an introduction to the subject.' It is now regarded as essential reading for all students of Marxist history and philosophy, and as a standard work of reference.

'It is far from being merely a handbook. It is that, and a history and a critical text too . . . and remarkably, the most accessible account of Marxism that we now have . . . it is difficult even to *imagine* a better book.' *Times Higher Education Supplement*

'undoubtedly the most complete and intellectually satisfying survey of Marx's and Marxist thought ever written' *Listener*

'a great intellectual achievement' Bernard Crick, *Observer*

LAW AND MODERN SOCIETY

P. S. Atiyah

'The Oxford University Press has done well to publish this brief, lucid and stimulating appraisal by P. S. Atiyah of English law as it operates in our society today. And it is refreshing to find that Professor Atiyah describes the law in action before he asks his questions. His study is critical, but not damning. Though Atiyah is careful not to state his own position and sensibly emphasizes that without judges educated by training and experience to handle and develop constitutional safeguards a Bill of Rights is unlikely to achieve its purpose, I find the conclusion to be drawn from his reasoning inescapable. It points to the need for constitutional reform. Atiyah leaves it to his readers to decide what they want. It is good, therefore, that the book is designed to be read by all who are interested; that it is written in a style which all can appreciate; that it is brief; and that it is modestly priced.' Leslie Scarman, *Times Literary Supplement*

'The author surveys the legal system rather than substantive law and has views on judges, the legal profession generally, the way lawyers themselves regard law, law and the state and "Bad law". Throughout the text he tries to be fair where there are two political viewpoints . . . the book is a stimulating introduction to the legal system for the intelligent layman.' *Solicitors Journal*

An OPUS book

THE ENFORCEMENT OF MORALS

Patrick Devlin

Since we live in a secular society, a law can no longer be justified on religious grounds. The law is concerned solely with the *facts* of common morality, rather than with any philosophical or religious conception of how it ought to be; and what the law-maker must ascertain is not the true belief but the common belief.

'the discussion in every case is brilliant, sophisticated and original.' Barbara Wootton, *Observer*

'Lord Devlin has tackled the subject in a clear, penetrating and lively style which will appeal to lay readers.' *The Times*

CAPITALIST DEMOCRACY IN BRITAIN

Ralph Miliband

How has Britain succeeded in avoiding violent political conflict on a wide scale since the suffrage was extended in 1867? Ralph Miliband suggests that the answer lies in a political system that has proved capable of controlling pressure from below by absorbing it. He illustrates his theories with reference to recent political events.

'Miliband's special contribution has made him our foremost Marxist political theorist.' *New Statesman*

BUKHARIN AND THE BOLSHEVIK REVOLUTION

Stephen R. Cohen

For more than two decades Bukharin's career was central to the turbulent history of Soviet Russia and the communist movement: he made important contributions to Lenin's original leadership, and after 1917 was a Politburo member, editor of *Pravda*, head of the Comintern, chief theoretician, and for three years, co-leader with Stalin of the Communist Party. He was tried as 'an enemy of the people' and executed by Stalin in 1938.

'Professor Cohen, in this brilliantly written, meticulously documented monograph, has not only reconstructed the tragedy of a fascinating man ... he has also produced a classic study of the intellectual development of the foremost Bolshevik theoretician ... He has, in a word, achieved a break-through in Soviet studies.' *Observer*

SOVIET FOREIGN POLICY

The Brezhnev Years

Robin Edmonds

In this book Robin Edwards, a former minister at the British Embassy in Moscow, presents a dispassionate view of the foreign policy pursued by the Soviet Union during Leonid Brezhnev's eighteen years as General Secretary of the Soviet Communist Party. Taking as its point of departure the Cuban missile crisis of 1962, the book analyses the Soviet Union's ascent to super-power status, the complex negotiations of the *détante* period, and the evolution and subsequent erosion of the relationship between the Soviet Union and the USA.

THE RUSSIAN REVOLUTION 1917–1932

Sheila Fitzpatrick

This book is concerned with the Russian Revolution in its widest sense—not only with the events of 1917 and what preceded them, but with the nature of the social transformation brought about by the Bolsheviks after they took power.

Professor Fitzpatrick's account, widely praised on first publication for its clarity and for its historical objectivity, confronts the key questions: what did the dictatorship of the proletariat really mean in practice? And was Lenin's revolution, in the hands of Stalin, accomplished—or betrayed?

'A crisply written, lucid, descriptive, analysis from an independent point of view.' *British Book News*

'A lucid and indeed instantly classic explanation of the revolutionary spirit in its pre- 1917 and Lenin-then-Stalin dominated stages.' *Tribune*

An Opus book

INTERNATIONAL RELATIONS IN A CHANGING WORLD

Joseph Frankel

In this 'comprehensive and compendious piece of work' (*Times Literary Supplement*), Professor Frankel combines a description of the foreign policies of the major world powers with a fascinating analysis of the diplomatic setting in which such policies have to be formulated. He demonstrates the growing recognition of the need for some form of global or regional regimes to tackle the problem of *International Relations in a Changing World*.

Professor Frankel pays particular attention to the state powers of the USA, Soviet Union, and China, and considers the relevance of international institutions such as the League of Nations and the United Nations in the prospects for solving problems caused by the conflicts between states.

An Opus book

THE LIFE AND TIMES OF LIBERAL DEMOCRACY

C. B. Macpherson

This is a concise and lucid analysis of the changing interpretation of democracy and the accompanying changes in the ways it can be achieved. In tracing the background of current liberal-democratic theory, Professor Macpherson rejects the claims commonly made for the seventeeth-century Puritans and Jefferson and Rousseau as liberal democrats, and argues that liberal-democratic theory begins (and begins badly) with Bentham and James Mill. He explains how the concept of democracy became both embedded in the shifting ideas of social equality and increasingly dependent on the mechanism of capitalism, and points the way to a more participatory democracy which would give the ordinary man a self-fulfilling role.